PROBLEMS OF HEMISPHERIC DEFENSE

PROBLEMS
OF HEMISPHERIC
DEFENSE

LECTURES DELIVERED UNDER THE AUSPICES OF THE
COMMITTEE ON INTERNATIONAL RELATIONS
ON THE BERKELEY CAMPUS OF THE
UNIVERSITY OF CALIFORNIA
AUTUMN 1941

UNIVERSITY OF CALIFORNIA PRESS
BERKELEY AND LOS ANGELES
1942

UNIVERSITY OF CALIFORNIA PRESS
BERKELEY, CALIFORNIA

———

CAMBRIDGE UNIVERSITY PRESS
LONDON, ENGLAND

PREFACE

THE SERIES OF LECTURES included in this volume were delivered before audiences in Wheeler Auditorium on the University of California campus, Berkeley, in the autumn of 1941. Traditionally the United States has tended to regard the Western Hemisphere as a region for the cultivation of an American civilization which, though enriched by the general stream of Western culture, and made up of diverse racial elements from all parts of the earth, would nevertheless develop a distinctively American legal, political, and economic system. The present political and economic war is putting the validity of this theory to a searching test. In view of the danger to the Western Hemisphere arising out of this struggle, the United States, Canada, and the Latin-American republics are exploring the many and difficult problems of coöperation and defense. It is hoped that the present series of lectures will make some contribution toward our understanding of these problems.

T. H. GOODSPEED,
Chairman

CONTENTS

INTER-AMERICAN TRADE AND
HEMISPHERIC SOLIDARITY

———

JOHN B. CONDLIFFE
PROFESSOR OF ECONOMICS
IN THE UNIVERSITY OF CALIFORNIA

Lecture delivered September 17, 1941

INTER-AMERICAN TRADE AND
HEMISPHERIC SOLIDARITY

I DID NOT choose the title of this lecture. The words have a fine ring to them. They carry an overtone of solid home comfort and good neighborliness. It is always wise to examine such words carefully, to see if they have any meaning and whether the comfort they convey corresponds with objective reality. It seems all the more necessary to examine these words because there seems to be some uncertainty about them. The title I was given was "Inter-American Trade and Hemispheric Solidarity"; but the official University bulletin gives it as "Hemispheric Trade and American Solidarity."

As words go, solidarity is rather new. It seems to have come into the English language from the French somewhere about a century ago. The original meaning, as given by Larousse, has all the clarity and directness characteristic of French thought. I translate literally: "Solidarity is the state of two or more persons each of whom is wholly obligated on behalf of all the others in case of their nonpayment." From this primary meaning a secondary philosophic meaning has developed in the sense of "mutual dependence between men so that one cannot be happy and develop unless the others are able to do likewise." The connection between the two meanings is obvious enough. One has a natural sympathetic interest in the behavior of anyone for whose debts one is responsible.

The word hemisphere is even more delicate of definition. Literally it ought to be half a sphere; but what constitutes half a sphere depends upon where one draws the dividing

[3]

line. In this case it is between east and west. This, I need hardly remind you, is a political question of some importance. The President of the United States has recently called in a group of eminent geographers to advise him on the point. No exact definition appears to have been arrived at. Sir Thomas Browne, as early as 1646, reported: "The ancient Cosmographers doe place the division of the East and Westerne Hemisphere, that is the first terme of longitude in the Canary or fortunate Islands." My atlas still places the Cape Verde Islands and the Azores, practically all of Greenland, and almost exactly half of Iceland within the Western Hemisphere. But there seems to be less and less certainty about this boundary line. Perhaps the best we can do for the moment is to place the boundary of the Western Hemisphere at the eastern limit of the patrol system operated by the United States Navy. I confess to a little anxiety on this point since New Zealand, on my atlas, lies snugly within the western boundary of the hemisphere. If the patrol system should eventually reach the ports of western Ireland, most of New Zealand would still lie within the hemisphere; but if it were to extend farther, New Zealanders might find themselves, on a strict definition, cast into that outer darkness which is said to be characterized by "weeping and wailing and gnashing of teeth."

I am not sure, however, that the truest meaning of the word hemisphere for our purposes is not the anatomical definition which derives from "a very deep fissure running from before backwards, and dividing the visible part of the brain into two lateral halves termed hemispheres." I would like to emphasize the direction in which this fissure runs.

There still remains the phrase inter-American trade, which might seem easy to define, but which raises a certain number of questions. In the course of its evolution the word trade has acquired a variety of meanings. Among them I note one or two that seem appropriate to our subject. The tread or track which marked a beaten path early suggested both a way of life or occupation and the passage to and fro of visitors as well as merchants selling their wares. It also came to have the meaning of fuss, commotion, trouble, and difficulty, and this meaning survives in the Yorkshire dialect. Trading developments in the Western Hemisphere in recent months illustrate many of these meanings, especially the passage to and fro, the coming and going. Let us hope they will not bear out also the dour Yorkshire phrase: "They'll hae plenty o' trade on afore they mak' t' business pay."

Finally, the compound adjective inter-American needs to be looked at. The use of the prefix inter- rather than intra- is perhaps significant. We are concerned with trade not within, but between, the American countries, including, I should perhaps remind you, Canada. This choice of prefix emphasizes the essential independence and sovereignty of all parties to the trade. We are concerned not with the formation of a great trading region centered upon the United States, but with the trading relations of a number of independent states. Trade between the Argentine and Brazil is as much inter-American as that between Canada and the United States.

This definition of our subject agrees with the declared policy of this country in ruling out the notion that the rest of the Americas might form an economic bloc dependent on the United States, a sort of *Lebensraum* into which the trade of this country might expand. It is hardly necessary to add that this definition, ruling out American imperialism, agrees with the declared policy of all the other American countries also. It is interesting moreover to notice that the prototype and forerunner of all these compound geographical expressions, such as intercontinental, inter-American, and even interstate, is the much broader term, international. You will remember that the fissure in the brain that leads to the formation of hemispheres runs backwards.

The subject I must discuss, therefore, might be broadly defined as the international economic relations obtaining between the American peoples and their bearing upon "that quality of being perfectly united or at one in interests, sympathies, and aspirations" which is the ultimate expression of solidarity.

Nearly always the historical approach to such problems gives both perspective and proportion. If we confine our attention to present circumstances, and still more if we project our own immediate desires and preoccupations into the problem, we are apt to get it out of focus. We need to remember that all the American countries, north and south, were developed by emigrants from Europe and in economic dependence upon Europe. The trading tracks that were beaten out led eastward across the Atlantic, not north and south. Not only the trading tracks, but the roads to higher learning, to cultural achievement, and even to political coöperation, led to London, Paris, and Madrid, and even to Geneva. Until just before the outbreak of the war, the coöperation of Latin-

American statesmen in the varied activities of the League of Nations was far more extensive and more realistic than their coöperation with the Pan American Union. This connection with Europe was especially clear in the case of the more developed Latin-American countries, as for instance the Argentine. It was more obvious in the case of Canada. London and Geneva rather than Washington were the foci of international commitments until the present war began.

It is necessary to recall these historical facts and bear them constantly in mind if coöperation among the American peoples is to be placed on a realistic foundation. The active, enterprising elements of Latin America are of British, German, Italian, Portuguese, and Spanish origin. They persist in the odd habit that foreigners have of preferring to speak and write in languages other than English. Their artistic and social standards are derived from the old civilizations of Europe. The capital for their economic development and the markets for their products have until very recently been European in great measure.

In the years between the two world wars the United States found itself rather suddenly and unexpectedly in a situation of economic maturity. So far from being dependent on Europe, Europe came increasingly to rely upon the strength of the United States. The processes by which this country became a creditor rather than a debtor country, with undisputed industrial leadership and considerable monetary and financial power in world markets, were accelerated during the last war. They were further strengthened by the disorganization of international economic relations in the troubled period between the wars. The present hostilities in Europe, Asia, and Africa have finally clinched them. There is no longer any doubt that the United States exercises industrial leadership as no other country has done since Britain's power was at its peak. Nor is there any need to emphasize the immensely strengthened creditor position of the United States and the power which this gives it in the financial and money markets of the world.

How does this great enhancement of the international influence of the United States affect its relations with its neighbors to the north and south? In order to answer this question it is necessary to look first at the recent evolution of inter-American trade.

The external trade of the United States has been undergoing very significant changes very rapidly, but perhaps not so rapidly as the international situation demands. It is easy to get lost in a maze of statistics, and still easier to select and group such statistics so as to obscure difficulties of detail; but if we look at the statistics carefully, certain major trends can be discerned. In the first place, there is a marked change in the character of the major exports of this country. Cotton and tobacco are still great surplus commodities, but there has been a notable shrinkage of wheat and edible animal products. On the other hand, exports of machinery, petroleum, automobiles, iron, and steel have increased enormously. In the years 1901–1905 cotton, wheat, and edible animal products represented 45 per cent of the total exports, and the four leading manufactured exports, including petroleum, were only 13 per cent. In 1937 these percentages were almost exactly reversed, the

manufactures amounting to 45 per cent and the farm products to 14 per cent.[1]

Imports show complementary changes. Raw materials such
as rubber, paper, silk, tin, wood pulp, and wool become more
and more important. Following them come foodstuffs like
sugar, coffee, and vegetable oils, and even the lighter manufactures such as cottons and woolens.

These are very significant trends indicating that the industrial leadership of the United States is being reflected in its
foreign trade; but they move too slowly to cope with the
immense problems consequent upon the shift in its creditor
position.

In particular, they do not move fast enough to enable the
United States to cope with the trading conundrums of Latin
America. The Latin-American countries may be roughly
divided into three groups.[2] Nine of them, mostly the smaller
republics of central America, but including Mexico, Colombia, and Ecuador, are very heavily dependent upon the United
States, which is the main market for their exports. The percentages of some of their exports that come to this market
run as high as 90 per cent, or even higher. But, even including
Mexico, three-fourths of whose exports came to this country
in 1939, these nine countries account only for 25 per cent of
the total exports of Latin America.

At the other extreme are five countries—the Argentine,
Bolivia, Paraguay, Uruguay, and Venezuela—which among

---

[1] Cf. Arthur R. Upgren, "Raw Materials and Inter-American Solidarity,"
in the Norman Wait Harris Institute Lectures (Chicago, July, 1941).

[2] Cf. detailed statistics in *Commercial Pan America*, Vol. X, Nos. 4, 5, and
6 (April–June, 1941).

them account for nearly half the Latin-American exports. These great exporting countries cannot find in the United States a market for more than one-tenth to one-sixth of their exports. The Argentine alone is responsible for 25 per cent of all exports from Latin America. It sells in this market only one-eighth of its surplus commodities.

The remaining five countries—Brazil, Chile, Dominica, Haiti, Peru—sell roughly one-third of their exports to us.

We may sum up the situation, therefore, by the statement that from none of the five countries which export half the total surpluses of Latin America has the United States bought more than one dollar's worth in six of their exports. From none of the ten countries which account for three-fourths of the total export trade has the United States bought more than one dollar's worth in three. Only by counting in the near-by republics, most of which are small and almost completely dependent upon the United States market, does the United States manage in the aggregate to absorb one dollar's worth in three of the total exports of Latin America as a whole.

I have approached the problem as it relates to United States imports for very good reasons. Such an approach is a wholesome corrective to the view that concentrates upon the search for markets in Latin America. We are too apt to think of the countries to the south of us as a virgin field for American salesmanship. In this respect too many of us have not kept up with the changed character of international trade in recent years. There can be no fruitful trading relationships in a world where everyone wants to sell and no one wants to buy. The most advanced and powerful industrial and creditor countries have a special need to learn this lesson. The little countries cannot prosper unless they are able to find means of paying for the manufactures which the big powers are constantly struggling to sell them.

The struggle for markets, indeed, has finally reached the point where sellers have overreached themselves. In the years immediately preceding the present war, the Nazi economists, guided by the fertile if unscrupulous genius of Dr. Schacht, rediscovered the elementary truism that imports constitute the means, and ultimately the only means, of reaping benefit from international trade. They bought wherever they could and as much as they could. It is true that they did not pay for what they bought, or at least not immediately, but they bought—and in so doing they chained the economies of the smaller European countries to their own. This they plan to do again and on a greater scale, a world scale, if they win this conflict. If they do not win, the situation will be easier; but the British people, who in times gone by have bought heavily from Latin America, are fully conscious of the powerful bargaining instrument which the importing capacity of their great market puts in their hands. This instrument they must use to reconstruct their export trade, buying only where they can pay in goods for lack of any other means of payment. After this war the British will have lost most of the invisible exports—the shipping receipts, dividends, and interest payments—that in the past have enabled them to absorb a large surplus of imports. In the future they will be able to import only what they pay for by exports. Therefore they will bargain to buy where they can sell.

It is a mistake, therefore, for us here in the United States to approach the problem of inter-American trade from the export side. The whole world wants American automobiles, refrigerators, and calculating machines. Immediately after the war the whole world will want iron and steel and even food and clothing. The United States is now increasing its exports enormously. It will have no trouble in increasing them to any extent it may desire. That is not the difficulty. The difficulty will arise when it comes to paying for them.

This issue becomes very clear if one takes even a cursory glance at the development of inter-American trade since this war began. The United States has long had an export surplus in its trade with that group of important Latin-American countries which is unable to find markets for its exports in this country. The Argentine, Paraguay, Uruguay, and Venezuela buy more from the United States than they sell here. They would like to buy still more. Since the war they have bought more, a good deal more. They have also sold more to the United States; but their trading deficit has grown. Nor is this experience confined to the countries whose prewar markets were mainly in Europe. Brazil used to sell more in this country than she bought here; but now the situation is reversed. This is true of Ecuador also. Only those countries such as Bolivia and Chile whose raw material exports—mainly minerals—are needed for defense production have been able to improve their trading position with the United States at least temporarily. The others have taken greater quantities of United States exports, but they have been able to do so mainly because of loans from this country, not because we have provided them with larger markets for what they have to sell. There is, in the last statistics available, some improvement to be seen. In the first three months of 1941 the United States imports from Latin America were 41 per cent greater than in the first three months of 1940, while exports fell by 19 per cent. The rise in imports was largely due to increased purchases of wool. The fall in exports was due mainly to the national defense program in this country with its priorities and shipping shortage.

Of the loans recently extended, or authorized, to Latin-American countries by the Import-Export Bank and the Stabilization Fund, over one-half has been extended to the five countries whose exports to this country represent less than one-sixth of their total exports.[3] The greatest amount of these loans—47 per cent of the total—has gone to the Argentine. There is a very simple reason for this. Three-fourths of the value of the Argentine's exports are represented by wheat, meat, wool, linseed, hides, and corn. The reluctance of the United States to accept imports of this type has meant that the dollars to pay United States exporters for the automobiles and machinery they send to the Argentine have been provided by the United States government. Over half the trading loans recently contracted have been made to this group of Latin-American countries whose exports we are reluctant to buy. Another has gone to the middle group, including Brazil, some of whose exports, such as coffee, we do want. Only one-sixth of the loans has gone to the countries whose main market is in this country, even though Mexico, Colombia, and Ecuador are in this group.

[3] *Ibid.,* p. 105.

In other words, the extension of inter-American trade since the war began has largely been brought about not so much by the importing capacity as by the financial power of the United States. It is true that the return of prosperity in this country has brought, as always, a need for greater imports of raw materials; but barriers hamper imports from the most important Latin-American countries. There is as yet no reciprocal trade treaty with the Argentine, Paraguay, Chile, or Bolivia. The veterinary restriction upon chilled and frozen meat remains in force. No way has yet been found whereby the major exporting countries of Latin America can sell enough to the United States to earn the dollars necessary to buy what the United States sells to them. Therefore the United States invokes its financial power and lends them the necessary dollars. We should remember, however, that in the last resort the financial power of the United States consists of the taxable capacity of its citizens. We should remember also that financial obligations have never proved a match for importing capacity. Any country which has to choose between honoring its debt obligations and stimulating current trade will choose the latter. If the Argentine or any other country is faced after this war with the choice of discharging its debt to the United States or of restoring its trade with Germany and Britain, it is difficult to see how any government could choose the former and neglect the latter. It is necessary, therefore, to consider means by which this dilemma may be avoided.

In the long run there is no escape from the elementary economic necessity that, if the United States wishes to sell its exports to Latin America in increasing quantities, it must be ready to accept payment for those exports in the only way in which ultimately they can be paid: it must be ready to accept an increasing volume of imports. This necessity may be deferred for a time by investing the export proceeds in Latin America. This process has already gone a considerable distance. It is estimated that in 1914 the investments of United States citizens in Latin America amounted to $1,649,000,000 or 22.7 per cent of the total foreign investments in that area. The latest estimates are for 1932, by which time the United States investments had grown to $5,429,000,000 or 52.5 per cent of the total. Since then both the total and the proportion held by the United States have grown substantially. As this war progresses a large proportion of the $4,050,000,000 (39.4 per cent) of British investments in Latin America has passed and is passing into the ownership of the United States, which is also making great new investments, both public and private, in Latin America.[4] The new investments are on long term for the purpose of industrial development and on short term and medium term for the financing of current trade. Wisely directed, such investment enhances the producing capacity of the receiving countries. Standards of living rise. Production is directed into new channels and in some measure away from the specialized crops that depend upon variable export markets. New import needs arise which the United States is well placed to meet. But in the long run the question of payment arises in a new and aggravated form. How are these Latin-American countries to pay for the new imports and at the same time discharge the service of their increased debt?

---

[4] *Commercial Pan America*, Vol. X, No. 1 (January, 1941).

So far as industrial development, including the provision of better means of transport, raises living standards and directs productive activity along lines that enable complementary trade to be developed, the problem of mutually beneficial trade is facilitated. The United States is likely in the future to draw increasing quantities of industrial raw materials and even foodstuffs from Latin America and Canada. There are some products, such as tin, coffee, cocoa, bananas, and fibers, which are not produced in the United States. Other products, such as sugar, hides, wool, and tobacco, do compete with local production, but the deficiencies that now exist might be enlarged if protection should be decreased and rising living standards should increase consumer demand. Other products, such as wheat, corn, and meat, of which the United States is still a net exporter, encounter greater difficulties in inter-American trade, but are of supreme importance to the major Latin-American countries. Among the minerals copper falls into this group also.

The mere mention of these commodities—wheat, corn, meat, and copper—is enough to recall the great extent to which the trade of the Americas is linked with other continents, particularly with Europe. The agricultural countries send their surpluses of food and raw materials mainly to Europe. The United States draws its industrial raw materials mainly from colonial areas dependent on the European economy. Inter-American trade, therefore, gears into the trade of the Americas with Europe, Asia, Africa, and Australia. It is a link in a chain of trading transactions covering the whole world.

It is often urged that regional integration and a greater degree of hemispheric self-sufficiency might be obtained. There is tin in Bolivia as well as Malaya. Rubber grew in Brazil before it grew in Java. Therefore, it is urged, let us direct our investment and organizing ability so as to make this hemisphere independent of the rest of the world.

This is a tempting argument, as all versions of isolationism are tempting in a mad, war-torn world. The raw materials exist, and we have the capital and the organizing power. Why not use them?

The example of rubber, now a most important import to the United States, is often cited. The rubber plant is native to Brazil, but plantation methods, notably in the Dutch East Indies, have completely transformed the industry. Its renaturalization in Brazil encounters great difficulties, of which the dearth of suitable local labor is not the least important. Capital investment and scientific research will not solve the problem unless at the same time there is effective action to recruit and render efficient an adequate labor supply. Such action is dependent upon government action in the countries concerned. Attempts to insure it by pressure from foreign industrial interests are a fruitful source of international misunderstanding and even of conflict. The provision of equitable taxation and stable government is another prerequisite of industrial investment. Concern on this account has retarded the introduction of tin smelters in Bolivia and oil refineries in several other Latin-American countries.

It is, in fact, easier to envisage industrial development in hitherto backward countries than it is to carry it out. Capital must be imported, and this involves the risk of foreign controls. Labor must be recruited and trained. Auxiliary and supplementary industries must be established. Transport, banking, and government services must be strengthened and extended. There is no doubt that industrial development is desirable in Latin America, that it has already begun and will continue, and that, as it continues, it will increase the demand for capital exports from the United States. But such development is always a relatively slow and disappointing process. It cannot be conjured up in an emergency. We may be quite sure that for the years that lie immediately ahead of us, and probably for a generation or two, the main production surpluses of Latin America will continue to be agricultural and pastoral products. Trade among the Latin-American countries is very small. In 1939, the percentage of their exports to one another was only 5.7 per cent of the total. Their exports to the United States were 33.9 per cent, and to Europe 41.9 per cent, of the total. For the largest exporting countries the percentages were even more remarkable: the Argentine sold 8.4 per cent of its exports to other Latin-American countries, 12 per cent to the United States, and 75 per cent to Europe; Great Britain alone took 35.9 per cent, a greater share than did the United States.[5]

Under the impact of war these proportions were naturally changed somewhat. In 1940 the Latin-American exports to one another rose from 5.7 per cent to 7.5 per cent, their exports to the United States rose from 33.9 per cent to 43.3 per cent, and their exports to Europe declined from 41.9 per cent

[5] *Commercial Pan America*, Vol. X, Nos. 4, 5, and 6 (April-June, 1941).

to 29.2 per cent. The Argentine's exports in 1940 were 12.1 per cent to other Latin-American countries, 17.5 per cent to the United States, and 62 per cent to Europe, of which 36.4 per cent was to Great Britain.[6]

If the United States wishes to expand its exports to Latin-American countries, it has two chances of getting paid for them. It can accept payment directly by increasing its imports from these areas, or it can assist in the restoration of a multi-lateral world trading system by which triangular payments may be made. It is of course highly desirable that search shall be made for all possible means of extending trade that does not compete with production in the United States. It is also desirable to foster industrial development in the Latin-American countries so that they may raise their standards of living and thus provide better markets for manufactured goods. But capital investment for this purpose must ultimately be paid for, and it can be paid for only by increased exports. In the long run, therefore, the problem of inter-American trade comes down to the question of enlarging the outlets for Latin-American exports. As far as we can see ahead, these exports are likely to consist in large part, for some time to come, of wheat, meat, corn, copper, and similar products which the United States is reluctant to buy.

The easiest way to solve these problems of inter-American trade is to restore multilateral trade on a world-wide basis. The surest way to destroy hemispheric solidarity indeed would be an attempt to force inter-American trade into a hemispheric regionalism. Latin America is more dependent upon Europe than it is upon the United States, or than Europe

[6] *Ibid.*

is upon Latin America. If we take the Western Hemisphere countries as a whole, including the United States and Canada, their mutual trade absorbs only 39 per cent of their total exports. The corresponding figure of regional self-sufficiency for Europe is 64 per cent.[7] Much less dislocation would be caused within Europe if regional self-sufficiency should be attempted by isolation from the rest of the world than would be caused in this hemisphere if the European market should be closed to it.

We delude ourselves if we think that hemispheric solidarity can be achieved by a regional development of inter-American trade. Trade can flow fully and freely between North and South America only if it is part of a multilateral trading process by which South American meat and wheat flow to Europe, European countries export to their colonial areas, and the colonies export raw materials to the United States, which can then close the chain of transactions by exporting its manufactures to its southern neighbors.

This conclusion, which appears inescapable from any survey of the economic organization and trading possibilities of the Americas, is not in conflict with the attempts now being made to expand inter-American trade, or in criticism of them. It is not only entirely desirable, but inevitable, that such expansion shall be sought. The more that complementary trade can be developed, the better for all the countries concerned. It would be foolish indeed to neglect the possibilities of expanding trade with our immediate neighbors until such time as wider trading connections become possible again. There is a very strong case, not only for expanding trade, but also for

---

[7] A. R. Upgren, *op. cit.*

extending financial support in this emergency to those countries whose normal export outlets have been shut off by war conditions. Even if there should be some financial risk in this extension of our commitments, it should be undertaken since "defense is of more importance than opulence."

We should, on the other hand, be very clear that the cultivation of closer economic relations with our good neighbors to the north and south cannot in itself be an adequate solution of their problems or ours. It is a highly important stage in the preservation and expansion of world trade; but it is not a feasible alternative to world trade even for us, and still less for them.

I suspect that the same reasoning holds true for other aspects of hemispheric solidarity, but of the economic aspect there can be little doubt. Attempts to force inter-American trade quickly into a framework of regional self-sufficiency would be the best way to destroy the solidarity of this western hemisphere. The simplest, most effective, and most enduring way to expand inter-American trade when this emergency ends is to develop it as an essential part of the restoration of world trade. This is the firm policy that has been and is being steadily pursued by the Secretary of State. Through all the discouragements and setbacks of recent years Mr. Hull has never wavered in his conviction that the path to peace lies through the establishment of freer trading relations, conducted multilaterally on the basis of equal trading opportunity, seeking no preferences or regional exclusiveness. The reorganization of world trade along these lines offers ample scope for greatly augmented inter-American trade and at the same time for inter-American coöperation in working toward a greater goal. It is out of such coöperation that mutual understanding is born and solidarity is achieved.

THE AXIS ADVANCE GUARD
IN LATIN AMERICA

———

RUSSELL H. FITZGIBBON
ASSISTANT PROFESSOR OF POLITICAL SCIENCE
IN THE UNIVERSITY OF CALIFORNIA

Lecture delivered September 24, 1941

THE AXIS ADVANCE GUARD
IN LATIN AMERICA

WE IN THIS nation have been afflicted with a curious sort of international astigmatism of late years. It is perhaps not apt to say that we have been unable to see beyond our noses, but certainly the vision of millions in this country has been limited by horizons surveyed only in terms of experience. "Nothing new under the sun," "It can't happen here," "Democracy is of course the ultimate way of life," "Dictatorships can't last"—these and a dozen other glib and easy generalizations have been the refuge of all too many persons incapable of facing and thinking through a hard set of facts, or unwilling to do so. The fact remains that the sun is constantly shining down on new things, that an efficient corps of Nazi *saboteurs* may now be demonstrating that it *is* happening here, that there has yet been no final choice between democracy and dictatorship as the final political philosophy and way of life. If it be heresy to be agnostic in such regards, then we are better off heretics; at least we shall be realists.

When in 410 A.D. Rome fell before the Goths—who, significantly, wouldn't fight according to the rules which some military Hoyle laid down for that day—it was not simply a political calamity to the comfortable Roman mind. The whole moral order was upset; men's reason reeled under the incomprehensible thing that had occurred; it was the onset of a chaos from which sanity and law and order might never be recovered, they felt. St. Augustine found his asylum in the City of God; attempts by others to rationalize were less successful or satisfying. If we, fifteen centuries later, try to find some escapist avenue out of the present dilemma, it may lull some individuals into an opiate sense of security, but sheer, solid faith in the inevitability of democracy is, to me, less comforting than a reasonable faith plus an arsenal of weapons and techniques and knowledge that can be used to counteract the forces that would overwhelm democracy. The voice of destruction is loosed in the world. If we listen only to its words we may be deceived and misled, as the Lindberghs and Wheelers seem to have been. If our ears are attuned for the overtones, we may be able to detect the deadly menace. In the latter case, it is not yet too late to do something about it—modern civilization has not yet entirely succumbed to the forces of nihilism.

The trouble with Hitler has been not merely fanaticism, but also ignorance. If he were less unaware of how nations have been conquered and empires built he would doubtless have been appalled at the breadth, temerity, and unconventionality of his plans and ambitions. Being ignorant, he had the courage to devise his own plans—and thus far most of them have been phenomenally successful. Conformity and predictability have been words foreign to his vocabulary, but the world has had difficulty in realizing that important fact. Our earlier postwar dictators—Stalin, Mussolini, Primo de Rivera, and others—lapsed ultimately into a conventionality of sorts so that long-range political forecasting based on what they probably would do was not impossible. Hitler has not run true to type. Even a dictator, we used to delude ourselves, has some regard for his pledged word; even a government with a broad, ambitious program, a *Weltanschauung,* if you please, must realize that its emigrant sons and daughters are permanently surrendered to the jurisdiction of the lands of their adoption; even a ruler so dissatisfied with a dictated peace treaty as to tear it to shreds at the first opportunity must still display some awe at the thought of overthrowing a system of nation-states now some hundreds of years old. But Hitler has successively and successfully flouted all these accepted canons of international organization and practice. Again we are forced back upon the conclusion that the vast majority of both individuals and governments are limited by the trammels of tradition, their own experience, and what is ethical because it is conventional. Hitler has been exceptional.[1]

The game the paperhanger has played has been one of juggling—a balancing act on a scale almost cosmic in comparison with anything preceding it. Its timing had to be worked out with infinite care. It has required a single-mindedness, an ability to reserve oneself, unconcerned with detail, for major decisions of policy, a willingness to break with the past, which only a superhuman—or a paranoiac—would possess.

Many commentators have pointed out that the Hitlerian revolution, if it were not to be diluted as Lenin's communist revolution was in the 1920's, could have no logical end short of reaching to the farthest corner of the planet. All of German

---

[1] Rauschning assures us that Hitler is impatient and contemptuous of such limitations. " 'Most people have no imagination. They can imagine the future only in terms of their own petty experience. They are blind to the new, the surprising things. Even the generals are sterile. They are imprisoned in the coils of their technical knowledge. The creative genius stands always outside the circle of the experts.' " Hermann Rauschning, *The Voice of Destruction* (New York, 1940), p. 6.

genius in organization would be called upon to bring about that extension. Every weapon and every method which experience could contribute or imagination devise would be necessary to achieve the objective. If we take a very brief inventory of what the German nation, confused and dispirited but no longer leaderless, had at hand on January 30, 1933, for such a campaign, we can safely conclude that it possessed at least three important assets: (1) a prestige as a great and powerful nation which, if temporarily and partially in eclipse, could at least be revived and built upon, (2) a mercantile and industrial establishment which, in a much more concrete way, supplied a springboard for world-wide enterprise, and (3) large and strategically placed bodies of emigrants who might be reclaimed as agents for and missionaries of the New Order, some of whom, indeed, would not have to be called back to an original allegiance, so little assimilated had they been by foreign bodies politic and social. We are concerned now with only the Latin-American area, and it is particularly the third of the assets listed above which calls for analysis.

It is impossible to determine the number of Germans, Italians, and Japanese[2] in Latin America. We should have to ask ourselves in the first place what is a German, an Italian, a Japanese. Are we to apply a legal, a linguistic, or a cultural and ideological yardstick? Statistics would be largely meaningless. It is sufficient to say that the total of the three nationalities represented in Latin America is several millions, with Italians first and Japanese last in numerical order of impor-

---

[2] I shall arbitrarily assume that Germany, Italy, and Japan constitute the "Axis" within the meaning of the term as used in the title of this lecture.

tance. The chief centers of Italian strength are the state of São Paulo in Brazil, Uruguay, and Argentina. By far the largest and most significant German colony is to be found in the southern states of Brazil (especially Rio Grande do Sul), where perhaps a million people by some cultural or emotional standard might be labeled German. Other important segments of the *Auslandsdeutsche* are to be found in northern Argentina and southern Chile. Emigrants from the Land of the Rising Sun have gone principally to Peru and Brazil. All three national groups are to be found to some degree in each of the twenty Latin-American republics, although in some their numbers do not warrant attaching much significance to the colonies. When one is engaged in any sort of statistical analysis, however, it is well to keep in mind that proportional fractions of the population as well as absolute numbers must be taken into account; 15,000 Germans in Panama, for example, would represent a greater fraction of the population than do the million in Brazil.

It is more pertinent to inquire into the concentration or dispersal of the nationals or descendants of foreign stocks. This fact will determine in large measure the degree of their assimilation by the populations of the countries in which they have settled. In case absorption has been considerable, recapture for an alien ideology will be correspondingly difficult. For two reasons, the Italians do not in this respect present much of a problem. More racially akin to the Spanish and Portuguese than are either the Germans or Japanese, it has been easier for the Italians to intermingle with the dominant elements in Brazil and Spanish America and to become one with them.

In the second place, the efforts of the Italian government to organize and retain the affections of this huge mass of emigrants have often been half-hearted and largely futile. The lower economic status and humbler occupations of the Italians, their frequent lack of social and educational attainment, their apathy toward political problems, have all contributed to the difficulty confronting the government at Rome in trying to retain their loyalty and enthusiastic support. But one must be cautious in generalizing too broadly; the Italian government has made some efforts, attended with some success, in keeping its Latin-American emigrants in line.

The Japanese, at the other extreme from the Italians, similarly present little of a problem, but for different reasons. Their racial dissimilarity from the Iberian groups is so great, of course, that any wide or early assimilation is out of the picture. The customarily lower standard of living, which results in greater economic competition with the nationals of the respective countries, would normally point toward increased friction, which would play into the hands of a home government wishing to use its emigrants for propagandistic purposes. The smallness of Japanese settlements, except in Peru and Brazil, however, minimizes the effectiveness of the colonies for such ends. Until recently little evidence had accrued that the Japanese government was concerning itself with the problem of organizing its Latin-American emigrants; Brazil is now realizing that she may have a local problem of large proportions on her hands at that point, however.[8]

[8] Robert King Hall, "Foreign Colonies of Brazil—A North American View," *Inter-American Quarterly*, Vol. 3 (January, 1941), pp. 16–19.

The Germans, as usual, present the biggest problem. They are, of course, less naturally assimilable than their European Axis partners, but can be absorbed more easily than the Japanese. If left to their own devices, the Germans might in time become, even in large numbers, a racial and social part of the dominant populations. They have uniformly displayed much less unwillingness to intermarry with and to learn the language and adopt the customs of the basic Spanish-American or Brazilian stock than is true of immigrants from, say, England or the United States. The qualifying phrase above, "if left to their own devices," gives the clue to a major headache which has plagued the governments of Latin America increasingly during the past half-dozen years. The Nazi government has confronted German émigrés throughout the farthest reaches of Latin America with not only an urgent invitation but an insistent demand that they submit themselves to organization and integration under the direction of designated and controlled leaders. It is a demand for an overseas *Gleichschaltung* backed up by all the calculating thoroughness and scientific precision we associate with Nazi policy.

In considering this clash of group on group a question must also be raised about the nature of the dominant population elements. Again we are faced by a diversity which makes generalization dangerous and at best only partially accurate. Not only do the hundred and thirty million people of Latin America show the greatest variations in racial composition, even apart from the contributions of alien colonies established in recent generations, but the social structure is, except in its broadest outlines, extremely complex. So far as ethnic composition goes, the countries range from the almost pure white stock of Argentina, Uruguay, and Costa Rica to the overwhelmingly Indian population of such states as Bolivia and Guatemala. Almost every combination of white and red, and in many places African black, that biological mathematics can suggest is to be found in one place or another throughout the several million square miles.

The dominant fact in the society of Latin America is the persistence of an essentially feudal base only lately affected here and there by the disintegrating influences of an advancing but still infant industrialism. The great landowning aristocracy has in many a Latin-American country furnished a conservative or reactionary influence which has colored educational policies, stifled social legislation, retarded industrial development, and, in a word, preserved, as best it might, a colonial social *status quo*. Consistently working with the rural aristocracy in the unfolding of political and social policy, the Church furnished another great conservative influence. *Latifundismo,* the problem presented by the great landed estates, was attacked occasionally by reform groups—who often had an inadequate social foundation—but the more successful, if less spectacular and obvious, assault on the established social order has come from the beginnings of industrialism in such countries as Chile, Argentina, and Mexico. This development, coming almost entirely since World War I, has bred an embryonic urban proletariat which, in centers like Santiago, Buenos Aires, Montevideo, and Mexico City, furnished fertile soil for alien ideologies such as communism, socialism, anarchism, and syndicalism. A by-product of industrialization was the growth and strengthening of the commercial and professional, that is to say, the middle, classes. Intellectual activity has always been prominent in the public life of the other America, and the poets and philosophers, or at least the persons with the mental outlook of those categories, have registered an impact of no small importance as a factor in the sociocultural composition of Latin-American life.

This, in a thumbnail sketch, is the social milieu in which the efforts of Berlin, and to a far lesser extent, Rome, have been exerted. Many elements in the picture played directly into the hands of the modern Machiavellis who understood the situation and were, of course, unscrupulous enough to take full advantage of it. For one thing, almost no country in Latin America is socially or culturally well integrated. The nascent industrialism, with its inevitable and profound challenge to the traditional feudalism, has intensified the customary divisions within Latin-American society. It has caused mutual group distrusts, suspicions, and friction that have been exploited to the fullest by Hitler and his advisers. The desire of the various populations to lift themselves, almost by their bootstraps, as it were, to better standards of living in the face of monocultural, or at least very narrow, economies which put them peculiarly at the mercy of world markets, made them more than normally susceptible to the siren lure of Nazi trade proposals and promises. The somewhat artificial and occasionally doctrinaire character of Latin-American intellectual activity has at times offered little defense against the spurious but facile philosophizing of Nazi leaders.

With this stage setting, let us turn to some consideration of the methods, objectives, and success of, and the reaction to and defense against, Nazi efforts in Latin America. It must be remembered that while, by the canons of an archaic neutrality, we in this country are still supposedly impartial bystanders, actually we are nonbelligerent and morally we participate very actively in the conflict. This necessarily colors one's point of view. "Good" and "bad" influences and purposes are subjective and relative terms. Judgments depend, very humanly, upon whose ox is gored. If one could see with the perspective of a Martian he might view the whole situation more dispassionately, but we live and think and speak in a world which science is constantly narrowing, and, even if we would, we cannot escape the frantic immediacy of events. It was never more true that "the world is too much with us."

The growth of Nazi infiltration into Latin America has been obvious; its birth was far less conspicuous. Indeed, the future historian of the movement may be hard put to it to uncover the first faint beginnings of attention to the America down under. Certain it is that the first Nazi agents were trying to sell their own brand of conformity to their German compatriots in Latin America before Hitler came into power at the end of January, 1933. After that date the going was easier.

By the early summer of 1933, if we give credence to Hermann Rauschning's account, Hitler's ideas about Nazi penetration of Latin America were definite even though plagiarized.[4] "If ever there is a place," Hitler is quoted as saying, "where democracy is senseless and suicidal, it is in South America." Brazil, Argentina, Bolivia, and Mexico loomed

---

[4] Rauschning, *op. cit.*, pp. 61–67.

particularly large on his Latin-American horizon, but Germany had "a right to [the whole] continent, for the Fuggers and Welsers had possessions there." The inestimable gifts which the Third Reich could bestow on Latin America would be capital, a spirit of enterprise, and the Nazi philosophy. It would, of course, be necessary to play both ends against the middle—to appeal to "good society" on grounds of loyalty and conservatism and simultaneously to exploit the Indians and *mestizos* with revolutionary doctrine. "Our weapons are not visible ones. Our *conquistadores* . . . have a more difficult task than the original ones, and for this reason they have more difficult weapons." All the difficulties of the Reich would be solved (!) if only Mexico could be brought within the German orbit, Mexico—"the best and richest country in the world with the laziest and most dissipated population under the sun." It could be "got" for a paltry couple of hundred millions, "but these official donkeys [the German Foreign Office] only pull when they have the old refuse cart behind them. Because a thing has never been done before, they think it can't be done now."

Thus Hitler in 1933 and 1934. If the man's ideas were grandiose, the realization of them was anything but visionary. Organization of the Latin-American areas—prospective *Gaue* in the Nazi scheme of things, perhaps—went on apace. The early activity was conducted largely through the channel of the traditional diplomatic establishments, vastly enlarged and energized of course.[5] The limitations of such methods soon

---

[5] The German embassy at Rio, for example, ultimately came to have about two hundred employees in contrast to the approximately forty at the United States embassy there.

became apparent, however, and other means of pursuing organizational objectives supplemented (but did not supplant) the original ones. The whole complex party structure of the N.S.D.A.P. was adapted to German-inhabited portions of Latin America. This meant establishing the same sort of *de facto* dualism for those territories as had been implanted in the Reich itself, the existence side by side of the legal and official organs of government and the agencies of the sole remaining political party. The latter, of course, had attained a position of preëminence and power fully comparable to that of the Fascist party in Italy, even if the Nazis had not to the same extent labored to find some juristic formula to describe the party-state relationship. Just as the party in Germany has reached out its tentacles to touch and control almost every aspect of life and activity, so the Nazi organization in strongly German-populated Latin-American sections became almost unbelievably ramified. *Gauleiter* and *Stützpuntleiter* ("secondary defense leaders"), *jefes* of this and that, units of the *Camisas Negras* (the hispanicized version of the *Schutzstaffel* organization) all became part and parcel of the ominous network of Nazi control. Schools, youth organizations, women's groups, commercial firms, newspapers, airlines, were all brought within the purview and influence of the party organization.[*]

The third step in the evolution of coördination and control—and perhaps the last step short of possible actual military control at some future time—was the subordination of the activities of both the diplomatic establishment and the party

---

[*] Cf. an illuminating chart of the extent and diversity of Nazi activities in Argentina reproduced in *Living Age* for April, 1941, pp. 140–141.

organization to supervision by agents of the *Geheime Staats-polizei,* the secret police whom we know by the telescoped term Gestapo. The Gestapo agent began to give orders to the ambassador and the party *Gauleiter* alike. The diplomat was likely to be steeped in the tradition of his calling, a tradition of which Hitler was so impatient, while party activity might become diffuse and heady with the enthusiasm of repeated triumphs rather than disciplined and controlled as the Gestapo could be relied upon to be. So far as the diplomatic corps was concerned, the masters in Germany found a certain advantage, indeed, in retaining some of the old school, pre-Nazi, career men as heads of missions, since they could be pointed out to skeptics, with seeming ingenuousness, as examples of how the service had not been Nazified.

This subtle reorientation of control was a logical step. It meant, as war came nearer and nearer, that supreme command of this important segment of Nazi endeavors was being taken over by the brute, animal force represented by the Gestapo. The change was symbolic as well as physically important: it represented one more, and a natural, step down the Avernus-road that Nazi policy, with its scorn for individual dignity, was inevitably following.

The non-Nazi world is continually asking about German methods and devices of penetration and influence, and almost as uniformly refusing to believe completely in their existence. No exhaustive analysis of what has been done in each of the score of Latin-American countries is possible or necessary. The techniques have varied like Proteus himself, according as the immediate situation seemed to demand one or another.

A brief glance at what has been done along certain lines in a few states particularly, with perhaps even briefer incidental references to developments in other countries, will serve to picture a sufficiently accurate and complete cross section of the whole undertaking.

Of the various types of penetration which have been available—and Nazi Germany has of course overlooked no bets—the most dangerous was perhaps the economic. Modern wars are fought and modern imperialism pursued primarily with economic goals in view. The sloganed *Lebensraum* is to be thought of not so much in the literal sense of giving 80,000,000 Germans physical room in which to live and move, but rather in the acquiring of a sufficient dominion for the working out of German destiny as a master race unstifled by any cordon which jealous nations might wish to draw around them—and that destiny is, in last analysis, chiefly an economic destiny. Economic penetration has almost necessarily been more open than other kinds and hence has been attended by less of that unwholesome fascination which has characterized Nazi efforts of other sorts. It has proved extremely dangerous, and the more so because a heavy flow of trade between Latin-American countries and Germany is, in certain ways, a more normal development than between them and the United States. It is beyond the scope of this paper, however, to attempt any analysis of the "trade drive" the Nazis have waged in Latin America, a drive which, while greatly dulled by two years of warfare with the seas chiefly under the control of Britain, has not been entirely withdrawn as a weapon of penetration.

What may be called political penetration consists in the exertion of pressure, by intimidation or cajolery, on the public officials of the Latin-American national or local governments. It has been the military establishments of one state or another that have felt this influence most heavily. It required no great insight, of course, for the German leaders to realize the preëminence of the military in the large majority of Latin-American countries and to order their own plans accordingly. The Latin-American states in which military influence in things governmental has been completely and, presumably, permanently subordinated to civilian control can be counted on the fingers of one hand. Much of the leaning of the other states to the German military model is a natural result of the many military missions which Germany has had in Latin-American countries in years past. Evidences of German training, even down to the style of uniform and the types of equipment, are to be found in more than a few Latin-American states. In Chile, for example, the army leans very heavily in that direction although the navy has inclined toward the English as a model and mentor; this divergence in the inclinations of the branches of the armed forces has its counterpart, although less sharply focused, in the respective sentiments of those branches in other countries. The irony of the situation lies in the fact that in countries where the threat to the established political order has traditionally come from the possibility of internal revolution rather than from attack by some overseas enemy an army is of greater importance than a navy; in some countries, even sea-bounded ones, the latter is of no more consequence than the fabled Swiss navy.

War Minister Dutra of Brazil is reputedly strongly pro-Nazi in his sympathies and hence in his influence on the Vargas régime. High army officers in Brazil, Argentina, and other important Latin-American countries have been given decorations and other marks of favor by the *Reichswehr*. Carefully selected young officers have had military scholarships in Germany. General Kundt of the German army made the business of military advising pay handsomely when a few years ago he directed the Bolivian armies—not too successfully, it must be admitted—in their war with Paraguay at an annual salary alleged to be $120,000.

The military aspect of Axis political penetration has had its dog days, however. The only important recent influence of that sort has been the large Italian military mission maintained in Bolivia. Heir to most of the Axis activity of this kind was the United States, which, by a recent count, maintains military, naval, or aviation missions in twelve of the Latin-American states.

If Nazi penetration is to be categorized, some of the activity of the diplomatic officials must necessarily fall in the political bracket. The press repeatedly gives us illustrations. We read of the sensation created by the discovery that an attaché was found carrying a portable radio transmitter from Argentina to Peru as "diplomatic mail"; of the flight of Gottfried Sandstede, embassy attaché at Buenos Aires, to Germany via Brazil when he was wanted for questioning by Argentine officials; of the efforts of Otto Reinebeck, minister to the Central American governments, to disrupt the Havana Conference. This tack, too, has had its risks. Ernst Wendler, German minister to Bolivia, was last July declared *persona non grata* for alleged complicity in a plot to overthrow the Bolivian government, and the papers have in recent weeks repeatedly forecast the imminent repetition of the step by Argentina in regard to the German ambassador, Edmund von Thermann. The exequaturs of almost dozens of consuls, of course, have been revoked, the southern republics following the lead of the United States in that respect some months ago. A diplomatic visa is no longer the broad blanket of immunity and the open sesame that it formerly was.

Still another activity which might be designated as political penetration is the work of the Germans in organizing and encouraging pseudo-political parties and pressure groups in the Latin-American countries. Most of these, it must be confessed, have had only a nuisance value, but they have served to muddy the waters and divert attention from the main and simple issues. Typical examples have been the *Partido Nacional de Salvación Pública* and the *Movimiento Nacional de Vanguardia* in Mexico, the so-called Green Arrow organization, a secret, terroristic group in Brazil; the *Vanguardia Popular Socialista* in Chile, and others. The most famous of these quasi-national, or at least non-German, agencies has been the notorious *Falange Española,* but since its activity has been less in the orthodox political field and more in the "cultural" arena it deserves a word of comment on a later page. On the whole, however, in regard to all these techniques, it is easy to confuse the smoke of political penetration with the fire behind it—difficult, that is, to say how much danger really characterizes it. The threat of Nazi-engineered *coups d'état* by which native puppet governments might be set up, for example, has perhaps been overrated. This danger should not be dismissed too lightly, however; it was allegedly imminent in Uruguay in June, 1940, and the German effort in Iraq a few months ago may have been a dress rehearsal for others.

We may regard strategic penetration as another broad facet of the whole Axis onslaught. This aspect involved especially the development of a wide network of airlines and airports, many of them entirely indefensible economically, throughout the length and breadth of South America. It is common knowledge that the first well-established and commercially profitable airline in all Latin America was the Scadta in Colombia, a German concern whose planes were piloted by World War aviators who could no longer find an outlet for their talents in their mother country. Scadta established an enviable reputation and in time was followed by Sedta in Ecuador, Condor in Brazil, Lufthansa Peru, Lloyd Aero Boliviano in Bolivia, and others. The connections with the Axis capitals, via the humps of Brazil and Africa, were frequent, and were spectacularly used.

The potential threat of these airlines, especially those in northern South America,[7] to the Panama Canal was so obvious, even discounting the more hair-raising elaborations in the Sunday supplements, that the State Department could not remain oblivious to the danger. The result was a clever and

---

[7] President Roosevelt cited instances in his broadcast on September 11. The somewhat peculiarly arranged Quilmes airport, operated by Condor just outside of Buenos Aires (as well as other fields scattered strategically), has been asserted to be a disguised and potential Nazi air base.

so far eminently successful campaign of freezing out the German-owned or German-controlled firms in favor of national concerns of the countries involved or of United States airlines or their subsidiaries. To take but one example as illustrative of the trend, Scadta properties and operations in Colombia were taken over some months ago in a well-timed and neatly planned and executed coup. Succeeding Scadta has come the nominally nationalized Avianca, in which, however, Pan American Airways has exerted much influence. The same step has been taken in other South American countries, so that one by one the links of the Nazi air nexus have been broken or isolated until very few air miles now remain to the Germans. Whether it is through Pan American Airways directly or through Panagra or Pan American–Grace, the star of American commercial aviation in Latin America is definitely in the ascendant. It is one of the most clear-cut and dramatic instances of the dulling of the weapons of the Axis in the other America.

Not the most important or dangerous but definitely the most theatrical and alarming phase of Axis penetration has been what may be termed the cultural and ideological. The sharp clash of ideologies has been clearly focused and the significance of this kind of threat has had a powerful appeal to citizenries that take their democracy as seriously as we traditionally do in this country, as well as to those democrats by conviction who are found in almost all the Latin-American countries. Haya de la Torre, than whom there probably has been no more noted Yankeephobe in all Latin America in recent years, was lately quoted as saying: "The present struggle is a true world war, not a conflict of economic empires, of purely mercantile rivalry, like the 'World' War of 1914. It is motivated by a fanatic philosophy, a creed which destroys in the name of divinity."[8]

It cannot be emphasized too strongly that the lack of social homogeneity, and in some sections and among some groups only the rudimentary development of what, for want of a better term, we call patriotism, are factors which on this front have played directly into Nazi and Fascist hands. Loyalty to social and economic classes often took precedence over a broader and less tangible nationalism. Members of the long-lived social-economic-political aristocracy have sometimes given only lip service to the democratic ideal that has all but universally been formally espoused in Latin America. Consequently, representatives of the group that was the traditional repository of political power were often strongly attracted by the basic Nazi political doctrine of monopoly and exclusiveness. The cult of the elite appealed powerfully to them. What they blindly overlooked, and what the Germans thankfully permitted them to overlook, was the other fundamental Nazi concept of Nordic superiority and the attitude of scorn for mixed races or, as the Germans sometimes called them, bastard breeds. This partly morbid, partly selfish inclination to an alien philosophy that apparently subserved their own class goals, especially since those objectives were being threatened by the ferment of a changing society, made the Latin-American aristocracies good soil for Nazi ideological seed.

---

[8] Víctor Raúl Haya de la Torre, "Latin America Fears Invasion," *Living Age,* Vol. 359 (October, 1940), p. 147.

The cultural and ideological appeal to Latin America was naturally varied as the circumstances of place and group demanded. Some situations called for a plea based on a positive, dynamic, constructive, and, withal, conservative, doctrine; others required the preachment of a frankly revolutionary dogma. Scruple and consistency were of course held to be the attributes of weaklings. The propagandistic efforts of the Nazis in Latin America, as elsewhere, have in general had two aims: the securing of a disciplined conformity and fanatic devotion on the part of all Germans, and the converting or paralyzing of those of potentially hostile points of view. The need for thorough regimentation of all Germans, whether they were willing or not, except for the post-Hitlerian exiles, was taken as a matter of course. For some, the acceptance of the Nazi program is no doubt merely the ritual of compliance. I recall that when I stayed for a short time in a German *pensión* in Guatemala City somewhat more than three years ago, several of the teachers in the German school across the street would, on coming into the *pensión* dining room for their meals, take the opportunity to flick an imaginary fly from an ear and then extend the arm upward in a continued gesture toward the picture of Hitler on the wall, all done with a studied casualness. The "Heil" was imaginable even if not audible.

German schools in many areas did yeoman work. In Brazil, for example, a country which prides itself on being even more of a melting pot than the United States, German-manned and -controlled schools, using German speech, books, methods, and of course objectives, were long permitted in the large colonies in the southern states. The same use of German schools to further the cause could be duplicated on a smaller scale in a dozen other countries. Prior to the war, an increasing number of the teachers destined for these schools were specially trained at the *Ibero-Amerikanisches Institut* at Hamburg, directed for many years by General von Faupel, Hitler's first ambassador to the Franco government in Spain.

Another conspicuous channel for cultural and ideological propaganda has been the press. Many German and Italian papers flourished locally in various Latin-American countries and with rare exceptions they were brought within the orbit of Nazi or Fascist control. Some Spanish-language newspapers, such as *El Trabajo* and the notorious *El Pampero,* both in Buenos Aires, were occasionally particularly blatant. Trans-Ocean, which the United States has officially regarded for some months past as a propaganda agency rather than a news service, has been especially active in supplying a German version of "news" not only to German papers in Latin America, but also to Spanish- and Portuguese-language papers, many of which could not afford to pay for a more impartial service. The Trans-Ocean office in Buenos Aires, for example, has maintained a staff of more than 100 persons and, until recently at any rate, has supplied 130,000 pesos' worth of free information monthly to 150 rural newspapers in Argentina. Along with these journalistic perversions the German and Italian governments have made many gifts of books to Latin-American libraries, schools, and other institutions. Radio broadcasting, quite thoroughly perfected technically by the experts at Zeesen, is a technique so familiar that it needs no

extended comment. Its narrow-beam distribution, its ability
to "jam" or drown unfriendly programs, its flawless Spanish
and Portuguese in very cleverly prepared programs make it
a potent weapon.

One of the most interesting and potentially dangerous of
the propaganda agencies employed by Hitler and Mussolini
has been the *Falange Española,* product of the Spanish fascist
régime of General Franco. The Falangist movement has been
a sort of pathetic stepbrother of the Fascist and Nazi crusades;
its basis has been no stronger than the poverty-stricken totalitarian régime in Spain itself. The danger lies in the fact that
it is a Spanish product, exploiting Spanish techniques and
temperament, and hence appealing deceptively to those aris-
tocratic and ultraconservative elements in Spanish America
which react similarly. Not even the ill-disguised report that
one objective of the Falangist movement would be to restore
the great Spanish empire of Philip II has succeeded in fright-
ening off its potential support in Spanish-American countries.
A recent crystallization of the Falangist movement, which
was becoming increasingly diffuse, was the organization of
the *Gran Consejo de Hispanicismo* under the direction of Ra-
món Serrano Suñer, brother-in-law and evil genius of General Franco. This Council of Hispanicism and the Falangist
movement behind it have been seized upon by the Nazis
as a convenient "front" and spearhead. The romantic and
sentimental appeal of a native Spanish self-styled *Caudillo*
succeeds in some quarters where a fanatic and sometimes awe-
some *Führer* cannot.[9]

---

[9] A good account, in almost startling detail, of Axis activities (including

Propagandistic efforts must have some more or less definite subjects, of course. They could not in this case be devoted simply and solely to a glorification of a somewhat vague Nazi "way of life"; they must be concerned with more concrete matters if they were to have any wide appeal. The chief subjects of Nazi propaganda in Latin America were arguments against any political or diplomatic rapprochement between those countries and the United States, arguments against any sort of economic monopoly by the "Colossus of the North," arguments against the "North Americanization" of Latin-American intellectual life, insistence upon the inevitability of German triumphs all along the line. More and more of an anti-United States bias has become conspicuous as the motif of the propaganda. This has appealed mightily, even if somewhat irrationally, to some of those Yankeephobes who had previously regarded the United States with a jaundiced eye. José Vasconcelos, for example, the embittered Mexican intellectual, has allowed himself to become a willing pawn of Nazi efforts. The bogeyman of communism has been lifted, lowered, and lifted again, depending on the current state of relations between Berlin and Moscow. Some strictly native subjects for propaganda have been exploited, when they could conceivably redound to Nazi advantage; thus, a certain school of thought in Argentina, probably Nazi-inspired, has been trying not merely to whitewash but to gild the memory of Juan Manuel Rosas, notorious Argentine dictator of a century ago.

Spanish) more than two years ago is to be found in David Efron, "Latin America and the Fascist 'Holy Alliance,' " *Annals of the American Academy of Political and Social Science*, Vol. 204 (July, 1939), pp. 17–25.

What can be said by way of assessment of Latin-American resistance to this insidious and persistent onslaught? In the first place, resistance is helped by the mistakes of the Nazis themselves. In their eagerness they have overreached themselves. Most Latin Americans fortunately possess more of a sense of humor than many Germans, and such fantastic propaganda claims as the one that Admiral Byrd's discoveries in the Antarctic were intended as a means of sandwiching Latin America between United States flags on both north and south, or the allegation that an important pagan church consecrated to Aphrodite was flourishing in the United States, strike the Latin American as patently absurd. The best natural ideological defenses the Latin Americans have are, on the one hand, a deep-rooted individualism which would strenuously resist regimentation, and, on the other, a generally growing spirit of nationalism. The latter has a long way to go, but it is successively reënforced as one flag after another of the small, free nations of Europe has fallen before the German Juggernaut. There are conspicuous examples of aroused leaders in public life in several of the southern countries. Witness Hugo Fernández Artucio, who vigorously and courageously pushed an investigation of Nazi activities at Montevideo a year and a half ago, or Raúl Damonte Taborda, who currently heads an Argentine "Dies Committee."

Dictators are nothing new in Latin America, but they are not and never have been dressed in Italian or German costume. Even the government of Vargas, the most ambitious experiment of that sort, falls far short of the Berlin-Rome types. Economically, the chief defense of Latin America consists in the bulwark of United States dollars, spent either logically or artificially.

The success of Axis vanguard salesmanship is debatable. The evidence is contradictory and confusing, much like the accounts of the six blind men who described the elephant. For example, a student of mine, the son of Vicki Baum, tells me that his mother on a recent visit to Mexico found innumerable and highly alarming examples of Nazi influence and even domination. On the other hand, a brother of Carleton Beals, a colleague of mine, says that on a several months' field trip in Mexico recently he encountered only one individual who had a pronounced anti-United States bias.

After all is said, there remains the almost inescapable conclusion that fire will have to be fought with fire—tricks plucked out of the Nazis' own bag and turned against them. Nicholas Murray Butler concluded recently that "we are learning how easy it may be to conquer and to rule the world if religion and morals are thrown to the winds and if the whole of the world's instrumentalities in the making and use of armed force are confined to the governments of the ruling despots."[10] We may avoid this pessimistic judgment if large enough segments of official and public opinion in the twenty-one "neutral" New World states learn in good time certain basic truths: (1) Hitler draws no distinction among the types of war that he wages; it may be economic, diplomatic, propagandistic, military, but it is all war; to conclude otherwise is to show the blindness of some of our leading isolationists.

---

[10] *Liberty, Equality, Fraternity* (An address delivered at . . . Southampton, Long Island, August 31, 1941; n.p., n.d.), p. 2.

(2) The Nazi program can have no other ultimate ends than complete world domination or complete collapse; in the former case some puppet allies (Italy and Japan, for example) might officially maintain the fiction of equality, but not even the most naïve person would actually substitute that fiction for the fact of subordination to the Nazis. (3) The ultimate battleground between these two great philosophies and forms of government, democracy and totalitarianism, may well be the Western Hemisphere, especially Latin America.

With but few exceptions the states of the other America are on the fence. The trite saying that nothing succeeds like success is nowhere more applicable than in Latin America. The success of the Axis advance guard will be determined not in the continent down under, where it operates, but in Europe. The fortunes of war will spell whether the Latin-American spearhead thrusts home or is withdrawn, dulled and ineffective. In the diplomatic, political, economic, military, and cultural fields the United States is practicing an aggressive democracy as never before in its history. We may or may not agree with its detailed manifestations, but there are increasing evidences that it is helping to turn the tide in Latin America. We cannot say that this program of ours consists merely in buying or bribing the friendship and support of the other twenty republics. Those states respond to bold, imaginative policy, and that is what Washington has unhesitatingly used in recent months. If the United States challenge to Nazism is backed up, further favorable response from the Latin Americans, the vast majority of whom would prefer to lean our way rather than Hitler's, may be expected.

In the European theater the Russian deflation of the supposedly invincible Nazi *Blitzkrieg* war machine has had a wholesome and significant effect on Latin-American reactions; the very fluid public opinion there responds with the delicate accuracy of a thermometer. The case of Russia, incidentally, has also brought home to Latin America with added force the sobering truth that Hitler's friends of today may be his victims of tomorrow. If the legend of the unconquerable Nazi continues to be punctured, this revised viewpoint will continue to flower. But the Latin Americans are still on the fence. Nazi prestige goes up with Nazi victories, and down with successful Russian counterattacks or bold stands by the United States.

If the twilight of Hitler's Wagnerian gods is to come, the Axis advance guard will already have experienced its own sunset. If, on the other hand, the German sun is only in its morning, Latin America will get the full, searing heat of its rays, as will the rest of this unlucky planet.

CANADA AND HEMISPHERIC DEFENSE

WILLIAM H. ALEXANDER
PROFESSOR OF LATIN
IN THE UNIVERSITY OF CALIFORNIA

Lecture delivered October 1, 1941

CANADA AND HEMISPHERIC DEFENSE

I CANNOT offer even the shadow of a pretense of approaching my subject as an expert. Nevertheless, I feel that my inability to qualify probably establishes a bond of good will between the lecturer and the lectured; for what have the world's experts done to deserve our confidence? You will be reading as intelligent critics of whatever may be advanced, and, let me hope, impartial critics as well; for my part, I shall be trying, as one who has lived most of his life in Canada, to bring intelligence and impartiality also to the discussion of a problem which for this country is exceedingly important. And yet it is probable that the vast majority of Americans do not even know that the problem exists, and, even if they do, they are vague on particulars and thus conscious of incompetence in the matter of a solution.

What is the reason for such a state of affairs? It is simply that no American ever thinks of any trouble as arising for him from across his northern boundary any more than he considers such a thing possible from the direction of Mexico. In the case of Mexico I suspect there is present an attitude of conscious racial superiority which it will take a lot of Good Neighborliness to eradicate; but there is nothing such present in the case of Canada. Any honest student of American history knows that in the struggle of 1812–1815 the inhabitants of Canada proved themselves, under the conditions of war then prevailing, the equals in courage, resourcefulness, and ability of the invaders. That is an experiment which happily has not been repeated, but twenty-five years ago Americans viewed, mostly with a kind of affectionate pride, the spectacle of a group of about 10,000,000 people providing in the course of the First World War armed forces of some 600,000 men, the great majority of whom were actually transported to the European conflict. This group of 10,000,000 people sustained a loss in dead of 60,000 men, to say nothing of the long toll of wounded. If the United States had suffered in proportion, 600,000 American boys would have laid down their lives in Europe. This Canadian army wrote its name large in history by several notable exploits of war, like Vimy Ridge and Passchendaele, and Americans glowed with pride over these achievements of North Americans against Europe's reputed best. And now once again Americans are following, I think on the whole with deep interest and profound respect, a second Canadian war effort; and this effort, despite all the ignorance and worse displayed over it by some persons in high places in this country, is again on a large scale, though of a different character from that of a quarter century ago. Thus, for example, Canada is literally dotted today from Halifax to Vancouver, 3400 miles, with camps in which tens of thousands of men have been trained or will be trained for the fantastic warfare of the air. At the end of the war those who survive will emerge with a superb and unchallengeable knowledge of the actualities of modern aerial warfare, a knowledge which no training can by itself provide.

Americans know well therefore the quality of Canadians as potential or actual men-at-arms, and, knowing this, they might perhaps be troubled about it, were it not for the fact that they know, first, that under conditions of modern warfare the bravery and courage of a small people living beside a large one does not count for much, and second, that no one on either side of the international boundary, with the exception of those incorrigible fools which each of the two peoples has to suffer among its citizenry, can think of any reason why the two nations should ever engage in hostilities. Thus with equanimity, but so often without knowledge, the average American regards Canada as a kind of large-scale summer resort, very pleasant to visit and capable of being made more so if Canadians would interest themselves in better roads; this summer-vacation land is peopled almost entirely by the Royal Canadian Mounted Police, the Toronto and Montreal ice-hockey teams, some picturesque *habitants,* and the Dionne quintuplets. If he is a Californian or an Oregonian, Canada is to him synonymous with British Columbia, or, if his horizon is greatly expanded, British Columbia and Alberta. If he is a Montanan, a North Dakotan, or a Minnesotan, Canada is just an extension of his own country, populated by people who face the same type of problems as himself and are just as furious on their side of the line at Ottawa as he on his side is at Washington, and for the same reasons. Michigan, Ohio, and New York people identify Canada with Ontario's southern fringe and the more westerly portion of the Province of Quebec. Finally, there are the Americans of Maine and Vermont, to whom the international boundary line was a species of political humor until the American State Department for some unfathomable reason decided in 1940 to make that political boundary an unnatural boundary, and cut off northeastern Americans from the pleasure of freely entertaining the citizens of what represented Canada to them, namely, New Brunswick, Nova Scotia, and Prince Edward Island. But of course actually Canada is British Columbia and Alberta and Saskatchewan and Manitoba and Ontario and Quebec and the Maritime Provinces, stretching in a great belt as the national coat of arms proudly, if a little obviously, proclaims it, *a mari usque ad mare,* "from sea to sea." And the escutcheon might add, if there were room, *et a flumine usque ad terminos orbis terrarum,* "and from the river unto the ends of the earth," and that would be equally true, since Canada stretches from the St. Lawrence and its feeders, the Great Lakes, to the Arctic shores where the earth's end once lay.

It is not the easiest thing in the world to get a good map of Canada here in the United States, not even around some universities; you might have better success with Borneo or Baluchistan. But if you are not of the breed that gets easily discouraged, keep up the search, and, having got your map, you may be rewarded with a good deal of food for thought. Far above the international boundary there lies a huge land area greater in square mileage than the continental United States, or at all events greater if Labrador and Newfoundland are included in the estimate, as for hemispheric considerations they must be. This discovery is likely to lead to complacency or to foster complacency already existing in the American mind; this huge land mass seems to constitute so magnificent a shield for America on the north. In the distortion of Mercator's Projection it looks more magnificent yet; but even in its normal reality it is quite impressive and reassuring. Here is the northern half of the continent, a broad belt stretching for four thousand miles between us and aggressors, filled with a people who, whatever petty things they occasionally bicker over with us, are friendly and well disposed to what Canadian politicians and after-dinner speakers—often the same, unfortunately—describe as the "great Republic to the south."

But let us stop a moment just there; the phrase of the last sentence was "northern half of the continent . . . filled with a people who are . . . friendly." But there is a catch; it lies in that word "filled." The figures for the Canadian decennial census of 1941 are about complete and point to a population of under 12,000,000 people all told. Of these at least 90 per cent live in a comparatively narrow band extending north from the international boundary from 100 to 300 miles. For while the actual square area of Canada is about 3,000,000 square miles, its usable area for purposes of human life and habitation is really but one-third of that, and conditions of populousness within that area are not dense except in the urban areas of Toronto and Montreal, while beyond that they exhibit denseness for the most part only in the optimistic Nevada sense of the term. Thus we must set a guard on our lips against vague statements about America enjoying protection behind the rampart of the land mass of the continent's northern half "filled" with a well-disposed body of neighbors. The filling is a good deal like that of the proverbial boarding-house cake, in which you are confronted not by a condition but a theory.

"But, of course," my presumed interlocutor will say, "while it is true that I was in error when I said 'filled,' the fact remains that, if the Canadian population is not numerous, it has this advantage for us, that these relatively few people stand essentially for the same things that we stand for in our view of the world and of the manner in which people should conduct themselves in that world. They talk the same language, they have the same kind of schools, the same ideals or even a little better of what constitutes justice and a fair trial at law, and the same kind of political institutions. Their newspapers are a somewhat subdued version of our own, and they prove themselves civilized by using dollars and cents to do business in. They also admit chapters of our fraternities in their colleges, they have public scandals comparable with our own, they use our slang, and are afflicted with all our leading religious and political taboos, while Rotarians and Kiwanians, Lions and Kinsmen, flourish unmolested on both sides of the line and conduct club meetings the similarity of which is amazing from Edmonton in Northern Alberta to Miami Beach in Florida or San Diego in California."

All this is true; and equally true is a good deal more that could be added, and in it a very important point is touched on. Despite the fact that French Canada, the Province of Quebec, represents a nearly solid block of people who are non-English-speaking for the most part, especially outside the cities, unassimilated and unassimilable to Anglo-Saxonism and priding themselves on that fact; despite the further fact that a large part of the prairie population are New Canadians of very recent vintage, it can still be said in a large way that America has, manning its northern frontier, a body of sturdy folk holding the same ideals as Americans do and living in the same manner in which Americans live, if not quite so luxuriously, and a people not unaccustomed to hardship, including that of a sure place on the first team in all world wars so long as the sentimental tie continues to exist that binds them to the World Commonwealth of the British peoples. It is a really fine frontier guard, and I am well aware that thoughtful Americans appreciate it as such and despise from the bottom of their hearts such troublemaking language as United States senators sometimes employ in moments which might be better occupied.

But my interlocutor, having got his wind again while I was talking, may very well come back and say: "It is true that the frontier guard while friendly to us and courageous is small relative to the vast figures of man power in which modern warfare is discussed, but beyond that guard lies again another great barrier against aggressors, the vast denuded Cambrian shield, the barren lands, and finally the Arctic ice and snows. Before ever the frontier guard of America, the friendly Canadians above the international border, can be reached, an insuperable natural obstacle must be bridged, and we rest our assurance in its insuperability. How shall the deadly miles of ice and barren rock be spanned? We are secure behind the no man's land of the Great White Silence."

Time was when that could comfortably have been said, comfortably because truthfully; but that time has gone by, even if its passing has been generally unnoticed. It was fairly interesting for those who had their eyes rather than their mouths open when General Italo Balbo, the Italian air navigator, came to Chicago's World's Fair with a fleet of hydroplanes, coasting down via Greenland and the eastern provinces of Canada to reach his terminal in American territory. But the interest of this was far transcended in thoughtful minds by two trips made in 1937 by Russian airmen, the one coming to an end because of fog at Vancouver, Washington, but the other finding its terminus at San Jacinto near Los Angeles after a 6400-mile flight under the command of Captain Mikhail Grumov, who is again with us as chief officer of the Russian planes with their forty-seven passengers which reached Alaska and thence Seattle recently. It is true that a subsequent flight went wrong somewhere along Canada's Arctic coastline, and the tragedy of this was permitted to obscure the other two amazing performances. But people forget, too, that under conditions of actual warfare the loss of a plane is nothing; if Britain sends out two hundred bombers to strafe Germany as far as Berlin, the loss of ten bombers is nothing out of the way. The point is, then, that it is perfectly possible for a flight to start on the other side of the world and arrive, perhaps 90 per cent effective, on the prairies of western Canada. It is true that such a force would get a most disheartening welcome if there existed on those prairies a force of veteran Canadian flyers provided with the world's best in airplanes, but if one may judge from the way in which, in the past, democracies have dropped every weapon when they have half-finished the job, it may be doubtful if 1950 would find such a force on the Canadian prairies with everything ready, not to the last button, but to the last screw bolt and cotter pin. There are no planes there now but training planes, and by 1950 the tool droppers might have forgotten to have any ready of any sort. Now if anything has been learned from this present war it is this, that long-range bombers, present in sufficient force, enable an army to escape the war of position by jumping over obstacles, whether natural or man-made, and by steep and swift diving to produce an effect as of long-range artillery far behind the supposed "front." It is the back of the front that modern warfare has made so vulnerable. With reference to Canada, and more especially with reference now to the west, an adequate force of bombers coming from the other side of the world could skip over the ice and snow barriers and the Cambrian shield of Canada, and yet again over the possibly tenuous Canadian defense, and drop down nowhere else but on the northern tier of states of this Union.

But my interlocutor returns at this point to remind me that the bombers are limited in their range of action through the necessity of their being protected by fast fighter planes in which distance of flight is sacrificed to speed of motion. Surely the reply to that objection is that while such may be the state of affairs at the moment of speaking, who can even guess at the extension of the fighting plane's distance capacity by the end of even another year of intensive planning and discovery, or by the end of the war, or by the end of another decade? It is possible, regard being had to the limits of the human frame itself, that we are fast reaching the speed limit of the fighter plane in miles per hour, but the moment that a limit is established there, inventive genius will tackle and will undoubtedly solve the problem of giving the fighter plane an immense extension of coverable mileage. And if anybody says that such a force, coming across the Pole from the other side of the world in wave after wave of attack, could not occupy effectively any large part of the territory of the United States by jumping over the Canadian far north and a dubiously existent Canadian airforce on the prairies, I merely suggest that such a person is crawling into a funk hole and pulling the hole in after him. The staff of the Royal Air Force may be presumed to include some of the ablest and brightest minds that Britain produces, yet they actually believed that Crete could not be carried and held by an air-borne invasion, and this may be the real explanation of their having occupied the island for six or seven months apparently without any serious attempt to establish more air bases on it. There are similarly many able people in the United States who discount the possibility of a successful air attack on this country. I do not challenge their ability, but I do not credit them with the possession of much imagination. Perhaps they even fly in the face of the facts; there were fifty things which the experts knew positively that air forces could not achieve. The Germans have done all the fifty and then some, and the British and the Russians are proving apt pupils, if indeed it was not the Russians themselves who first worked out the technique of aerial warfare as the Germans have practiced it.

But yet again the objector says: "You speak of an attacking force coming from the other side of the world across the Pole; from just what country do you anticipate that they will come?" That is a question that I do not propose to attempt to answer by myself; I prefer to send you, not back to your deceiving flat maps, but to your globular maps, and when you have got to your globes, just examine for yourselves what places in Europe provide the best departure points for a flight across the Pole to the land mass of North America. One thing would seem tolerably certain to everybody except those blind leaders of the blind who go up and down among us crying "Peace! Peace!" when there is no peace, and that is this, that any master of the European land mass who had designs on the United States might conceivably have his general air staff study the amazing Soviet flights of 1937. Before leaving those flights I want to register once again the idea that their astonishing significance in the way of potentialities has been handsomely overlooked.

A similar study could be attempted of the eastern air approaches to Canada; but there would not be quite the same value in it, because the wise foresight of those who are directing the defense of this country has secured an air base in Newfoundland and one in Labrador, and has occupied Iceland and Greenland, while meantime keeping a watchful eye on all adjacent waters. There are those who tell us that the occupation of Iceland is a ruthless act of aggression on the part of the United States; I would say that the aggression thus practiced is about on a par with that of a municipality (shall we say San Francisco?) which, faced with a conflagration involving its total destruction, forgets for the moment about the rights of property and dynamites ten blocks of houses to save a thousand squares. It may well be that the world should be run on the principles of the Golden Rule and the Sermon on the Mount, but for the time being I am personally well satisfied that those who direct our national defense should not be obsessed by any notion that it is so run.

Now let us turn away from the line that we have been following thus far and begin a study of the political status of Canada—we shall find it important to our understanding of the general topic. Again one is rather amazed at the popular lack of information and appreciation prevailing in the United States as to Canada's political situation in the world. It is far from my intention, however, to blame the average citizen for this shortage of knowledge when I call to mind the fact, which may have eluded your observation, that the State Department of the United States was unable to explain to the President and the other responsible heads of this country why Canada did not hand walking papers to the German consul general in Montreal the moment Britain declared war on September 3, 1939. In consequence, the telephone between Washington and Ottawa was finally pressed into service in order that the State Department might bring its political knowledge of its nearest and best neighbor up to date. It then learned what anyone might have expected it to know, that Canada is not subject to the legislation of Great Britain nor committed *ipso facto* by Great Britain's declarations, but is a member of the British Commonwealth of Nations, each member of which is an independent state capable of taking what action it will, even if that action should be contradictory of the policy of Great Britain herself. Thus the Parliament of the world's other U.S.A., the Union of South Africa, waged a long and bitter debate on the subject of entering the war at all, and the decision to do so was finally reached by a majority of eighteen in a total vote of about one hundred and fifty. The reason that Canada had done nothing about the German consul general at Montreal was that Canada was not at war with Germany when Great Britain declared war, and did not enter into that state of war until September 10 after the Parliament of Canada had been convened and had voted on the question. It is of some historical interest to note that, although a recorded vote was not pressed for, it was obvious that there were approximately fifteen dissenters from the decision. By this time the State Department at Washington had added, let us hope, a few supplementary notes to its budget of political information.

Thus the actual position of Canada in the present war differs from that which she occupied in the First World War. There was no question then that a decision of Great Britain for war obligated the dominions and put them also automatically in a state of war. But the Statute of Westminster of 1926 changed all that, and it became necessary for each member of the British Commonwealth to make its own decision in 1939. Ireland stayed out and her decision has been scrupulously respected to the great damage of Britain in property and the lives of gallant sailors both of the merchant marine and of the Royal Navy, but to Britain's lasting honor. South Africa wavered and its war effort has undoubtedly been hamstrung by the opposition party, who go as near treason as they dare but do not dare much as they are adequately watched. Canada, Australia, and New Zealand, freely choosing, very quickly threw their lot in with Great Britain, and from the dates of the resolutions of these several parliaments is reckoned their entrance into the Second World War. With this so far clarified that I hope no one will go from this hall in the curious state of bias or ignorance which imagines that the King of Great Britain has the inalienable right to compel Canadians to come and fight for him—while as a matter of fact the Queen is the only person in Britain who probably could, since she captured all hearts among Canadians as among Americans in her 1939 visit—let us pass on to consider the curious implications of the political situation.

Fundamental to a consideration of this is as definite a statement of the Monroe Doctrine as one can conveniently incorporate into this limited address. I take the following sentences from the memorandum prepared by Mr. Robert Lansing as counselor for the State Department under President Woodrow Wilson in 1914. He writes: "The Monroe Doctrine is in substance that the United States considers the extension of political control by a European power over any territory in this Hemisphere, not already occupied by it, to be a menace to the national safety of the United States. In 1823, when the Doctrine was enunciated, the dangers of the extension of European political power on this continent lay in the possible occupation of unsettled regions and in the conquest of the territory of an independent American state. Later, during the Polk Administration, another danger was recognized in the possibility of a voluntary cession of territory by an American state to a European power, and the Monroe Doctrine was shown to be broad enough to include this means of acquiring political dominion. The inclusion of voluntary cession among the acts of acquisition against which the Monroe Doctrine is directed introduces the necessary corollary that it may be invoked against an American government as well as against a European government." This is Mr. Lansing's succinct statement, and I make bold to say that it will surprise a good many Americans who think that the Doctrine is directed exclusively against European aggressors, to find that it could just as well and just as reasonably be applied against an American state proposing to surrender its independence to a European power. I imagine that it would be held to apply equally to any acquisition of territory in the Western Hemisphere by an Asiatic power. It is interesting also to find a little farther on that Mr. Lansing states fairly and squarely that it is a policy based on selfishness, and that "the author of the Doctrine had no higher or more generous motive in its declaration." This has been better understood in Central and South American countries than in the United States itself, and that is why the Good Neighbor policy, despite much camouflaging of the truth, starts out under a heavy initial handicap. However, our concern is not with them, but with another country, for the happiness and the security of which it was certainly not designed.

The reference is to Canada, which American presidents and statesmen generally, until the most recent times, have looked upon as of necessity bound sooner or later, preferably sooner, to become an integral part of the American union. The pages of American history bristle with harsh words and also a few unpleasant acts illustrating what I have said, and Americans who are sometimes puzzled over some show of Canadian hostility to themselves might do worse than read a fair presentation of their own history for an explanation. And because this conviction existed, the formation of the Canadian Con-

federation in 1867 was bitterly attacked in a unanimous vote
of the American House of Representatives—but that is in a
sense apart from the subject. This belief, however, in what
Professor Goldwin Smith called "Canada's manifest destiny,"
led American statesmen all along to suppose that the application of the Monroe Doctrine to Canada would be readily
settled on the day when the various provinces and territories
of Canada became states and territories of the United States;
as this day was likely to arrive almost any time, there was no
need in the interval to worry about the precise interpretation
of the Doctrine in relation to Canada. But I am afraid that
the near advent of that day has been chased off the scene of
practical politics by the exceeding maladroitness of the American wooing which continues down to the present year of
grace, being most recently illustrated by the exceedingly unfortunate and ill-advised statements of Senator D. Worth
Clark of Idaho. It is always possible that economic developments may cause the two countries to merge into one, but
loose and wild language on either side of the boundary line
is likely to make the marriage, should it come, one of con-
venience rather than love.

What has actually happened, of course, is that Canada, after
a long colonial and semicolonial tutelage, has become definitely and clearly an American nation, though its path to nationhood has lain not through revolution but rather through
the establishment of a gradual claim on Canada's part to independence and the recognition of that claim by Britain. I do
not say that everybody in Britain, even of the supposedly in-
formed political class, understands this, but practically every-

body of intelligence in Canada does, and that is really what matters. Canada as a nation maintained up till very recently her own ministries in France, Japan, and the United States. The last-named ministry functions, and never more effectively, at this very hour; that to Japan is very sick indeed, and that to France has, fortunately, under the present odious circumstances, ceased to be, though for some unfathomable reason a Vichy representative remains at Ottawa, but the principle was well established in the three cases mentioned. So it might as well be said frankly that Canada is a nation, even if a number of Americans cannot comprehend that nationhood might conceivably be reached by peaceful processes of development rather than by abrupt break in old associations.

But Canada is a nation with special affiliations; it is a member of the British Commonwealth of Nations, which perhaps better than anything else in the world today presents a hopeful study of a future League of Nations that will work. It is a member of that Commonwealth voluntarily, and along with other members of the Commonwealth accepts the person of the King of Britain as a suitable symbol of a certain identity of ideas and of aspirations. Hence Canada is an American nation very closely related to sister nations all around the world; and this certainly introduces a new factor into the problem. Canada has never taken her seat in the Pan-American congress, not because she is opposed to it, since in fact many thoughtful Canadians think she would be well advised to do so, but because she has the other connection which is sentimentally and historically strong. Perhaps, too, Canada would not care to be put on a parity with Latin-American states. And of course the United States, whatever the formal bonds of Pan-American union and the political advantages of a perfected Pan-Americanism, really has the same sentimental and historical ties as Canada, and privately finds them more emotionally satisfactory than the somewhat forced devotion to studying languages of Latin origin which few Americans will ever learn because actually they do not care to comprehend them, or to wooing the difficult and uncertain Latin temperament. "La donna è mobile" might well be adopted as the theme song for this projected union of souls. In short, Washington probably thinks Ottawa not so entirely dumb in her present *nolo episcopari* attitude toward Pan-Americanism.

The British Commonwealth of Nations, legally set on foot by the 1926 Statute of Westminster, has not been long in coming to a hard and brutal test of its significance and worth. The declaration of war on Germany by Great Britain demanded that the several members put themselves on record. Had sixty or seventy years elapsed between the First World War and the Second, Canada's decision might conceivably have been to declare her independence of the Commonwealth arrangement by nonadherence to the British declaration and she might thus have become a strictly American nation, but 1939 was too close to 1914 to allow even the possibility that such a course should be seriously considered. So Canada, an American nation, declared war on Hitler and all his works and on Mussolini and all his words a few months later.

Now here was something that the founders of the Monroe Doctrine and its expounders and expanders had never anticipated, namely, that an American nation not actually attacked in its geographical location in the Western Hemisphere should declare war on European countries and thus invite the struggle, if you like to put it so, to the shores of this continent, and create the possibility of conjectural Axis victors demanding as part of the prizes of victory some portion of Canadian soil. The United States did not after 1918 propose to involve itself again, if possible, in a "European" war, and never of course contemplated that any Central or South American country might embark on such a war. But Canada was an American nation, and yet, through its position in the British Commonwealth, it had declared war on the foremost military power in Europe and indeed, as it at one time appeared, in the whole world. Canada could hardly be stopped from doing so, and the sour advice of Colonel Lindbergh to Canadians "not to draw the United States into war because they preferred a king to a president" not only served to exhibit the Colonel's oversimplification of history and incomprehension of spiritual imponderables, but also to make the Canadian people more resolute in the course they had sorrowfully but with a good deal of conviction entered upon. I think we may say, speaking broadly, that everything that has happened since that time as between the United States and Canada constitutes the last great amazing development of the Monroe Doctrine, namely, that the United States will never permit Canada as an American nation to become either in whole or in part the prize of victory for any European power whatever. There is nothing neutral about the United States when it is a question of Canada; Canada must win, or perhaps we should say, more modestly, be on the winning side, or, if not, the United States would have to employ its armed forces to prevent any untoward effects arising from her losing. The easiest and most natural thing to do was to bet on Canada's winning and to contribute in every possible way to her so doing, and this is what has been done; but further, the recognized necessity of defending Canada from the aggressor by deeds and not words, should the worst come to the worst, has been no small factor in the shaping of national defense measures, no small argument in urging its necessity. As Mr. John MacCormac in his fascinating volume *Canada: America's Problem* writes (p. 15): "This is a construction of the famous Monroe Doctrine which must make President Monroe turn in his grave. That a declaration originally designed to prevent the establishment in the Western Hemisphere of new European colonies ... would ever be used to deny to Europe the right to strike back in any vital sense at an American country which might be striking vitally at Europe could not have occurred to him in his wildest dreams." Yet that seems clearly the point to which the Doctrine has now advanced, and it could not possibly have mattered in the end which party was in power in the United States when this happened; neither party would tolerate the occupation of Canada in whole or in part by a European state, because such a toleration would be the complete end of even the semblance of hemispheric defense.

I feel certain that the statement just given will probably be annoying to those Americans who feel themselves to be the present-day representatives of those men in the past, including a number of very distinguished citizens of the United States, who felt, as President Grant bluntly put it, that the annexations that the United States must make for her comfort and security should include "perhaps Canada if she is amiable or if she is troublesome and ungracious." In other words, a pleasant marriage with Canada if she smiled on her suitor, or a shotgun marriage if she didn't, with the remarkable spectacle this time of a shotgun pressed against the prospective *bride's* side. It may be that Americans, engaged on the vastest scale in history in the expansion of settlement and the erection of a gigantic industrial order, paid little attention to these words of Grant's, but Canadians heard and were distinctly not pleased. If wooing was to be the order of the day, I cannot think of any more maladroit lovemaking than that of Uncle Sam to Canada, only really corrected at long last by the great tact and the diplomatic international manners of Franklin D. Roosevelt.

There has existed often in the past history of the United States a feeling that the bull (or the bull calf, if you like) might as well be taken by the horns and Canada annexed in order to rid the country of the necessity of any further thinking about the implications of having a northern neighbor with European connections. Any annoyance such as I have suggested arises out of the fact that this was not done when the temper of the American people was adventurously imperialistic, and out of the realization that this temper has now passed away. After the tide of verdicts, official and private, against aggressor nations, the United States could not, without winning an obloquy comparable to that so justly meted out to Hitler, proceed by force or even high-pressure diplomacy to force Canada into the Union. Remember, I am not saying that she will not come in; but when and if she comes, it will be by "an open covenant openly arrived at." Dorothy Thompson in her syndicated column appearing in the San Francisco *Chronicle* of September 9, 1941, states the case simply when she writes: "We wish to maintain such relations with all neighbors contiguous to us on land that it is never necessary for the United States to support permanently a huge standing army. We see no advantage to the United States in further expanding its contiguous territory, and we see profound threats to our liberties and our prosperity in a situation that requires that we become a great land power with permanent standing forces." I believe that to represent American feeling on the matter.

It is clear, therefore, that in considering Canada and hemispheric defense from the political angle we must agree (1) that the United States cannot, having regard to the present antiaggressor, antimilitaristic spirit of its people, solve the problem by annexing Canada, and (2) that an independent Canada, voluntarily contributing in a most important way to an attack upon a European power, is perforce protected by the last expansion of the Monroe Doctrine against any consequences of retaliation by that European power of a sort which would compromise the territory of Canada in any degree whatever. It is not merely the point of military defense that is at issue here, it being admittedly easier to keep the interloper out than to try to cope with him after he is comfortably established in British Columbia or New Brunswick; the fact is that Canada's territorial integrity is the collateral for the very large American investment in that country. No American government will ever allow a European power to impair that security by armed intrusion on the Canadian domain. President Roosevelt has so stated categorically as recently as 1938 on the occasion of the opening of the new international bridge among the Thousand Islands of the river St. Lawrence, declaring that the United States would not stand idly by if the domination of Canadian soil were threatened by some new European empire. Mr. Wendell Willkie went up to Canada last spring and left the same impression with the Canadian people in the speeches he delivered there. It might of course be added that any attempt to attach Canada forcibly to the American body politic would bring down like a house of cards the Good Neighbor policy, since it would be made obvious that the power which could make up its mind to gobble Canada today might pass on easily to the absorption of Costa Rica tomorrow and that of Venezuela next week. That the capacity to do so exists, no one doubts; all prospect, however, of a happy Pan-American harmony in the future lies in a belief among the peoples of the Americas outside of the United States that she has no desire for any such acquisitional exhibitionism.

Passing from the extremely curious political situation, almost incredible except to one who has looked into it, one might readily embark on the economic question; indeed, on one single phase he might expend more time than the average reader or listener would tolerate, even though that time might be the most profitably expended hour in such a reader's or listener's lifetime. That one phase would be the immense expansion of Canadian manufacturing industry under the pressure of war needs in fields hitherto undreamed of in Canada. Canada has notoriously for many years been one of the best buyers of American machinery of all sorts, but I invite attention here and now to the very great probability that, by the time this war has ended, Canada will have perfected her industrial system and developed her body of highly skilled workers to the point that there may be a most alarming decline in purchases by that country of American-made machinery. There could be no rational complaint from the United States about such a result, since Canada would simply have been following for herself the lesson of that particular kind of self-development in which the United States has been so peculiarly successful, and secondly, because the United States would have been largely responsible for it by maintaining through its financial institutions an approximate 11 per cent exchange rate against the Canadian dollar. It is a matter of profound astonishment to me that people as able and intelligent as Americans are should fail to see that the operation of this exchange discount is simply to give the Canadian manufacturer an added 11 per cent tariff against American goods. It would absolutely pay the United States to bolster through governmental action Canadian exchange to parity rather than supinely to see its best customer forced into becoming self-sufficient in lines where American goods, especially capital goods such as tools, dies, and machines, have heretofore had the call in the Canadian market. And if anyone cares to ask what relation this has to the problem of Canada and hemispheric defense, one part of the reply at least is this: that Canada will probably decide to do her own arming for the future, full of pride in her new-found talent for making the intricate machines of war, and that for lack of American diplomatic handling of the economic situation she might, and probably will, use British standards and gauges, whereas the problem of hemispheric defense would be simplified if Canada and the United States used identical gauges and substantially identical equipment for field guns and the huge rifles of coastal defense. The fact cannot be overlooked by any thoughful observer that places like Toronto, Hamilton, Windsor, and Montreal present today scenes of industrial activity not exceeded in relative intensity by anything being carried on in the United States. I shall draw this brief section to a close by remarking that as a former Canadian now resident among you I can never cease marveling at the amount of talk and effort expended by American economists on the probably insoluble problem of establishing a satisfactory trade basis between the United States and South American countries, while the biggest trade problem of the United States at the close of the war will perhaps lie on her northern border.

It is now time to approach as a last consideration in this paper the application of all that has preceded to the question which most particularly concerns the United States of America, namely, the relations of the United States and Canada in hemispheric defense. I start from the point of development which we saw that the Monroe Doctrine has reached. The plain fact is that the United States is in a position where willy-nilly it must see that for hemispheric purposes the defense of

Canada is provided for. It is a game, if one may put it so, of truth or consequences; if you don't tell the truth and face its meaning, you must pay the consequences. Now this might mean that Canada, apart from such interest as she might have in maintaining her dignity as a self-sufficient nation of the British Commonwealth, could simply lie down and say, "American is bound in her own interest to defend us against all comers; why should we worry about defense?" and I have heard Canadians, some of them, say precisely that, just as I suppose it is often enough said in Central or South America. It sounds pretty mean, but this is a hard world, and if somebody else *must* do necessary work for you as a condition of his own survival, why should you do it too? But of course Canadians do have a decent pride after all, and ninety-nine out of a hundred of them have no intention whatever of sponging on the United States in this matter of hemispheric defense. The United States is very fortunate indeed, in my judgment, since a country cannot escape having neighbors, in having such a neighbor, so capable, so industrious, so self-respecting, so courageous, and so dependable in business transactions. She has no other such neighbor in all this hemisphere, especially when you take into account in addition to the qualities just mentioned the practically identical ideals of the two countries, and any military man will tell you that with a force of Americans and Canadians, backed with the proper material of war, he would fear no foe whether in shining armor dressed or in any other uniform. There is therefore not the slightest fear of the United States' being obliged to feel itself let down by Canada because of the pres-

ent status of the Monroe Doctrine, or of the United States'
being entitled to feel that somehow or other it has been
rooked, and that the Canadians have pulled a fast one on
Uncle Sam. Let us examine the facts.

In the first military service act of the present war Canadians
from 21 to 24 years of age were called up, and young men
as they reach twenty-one are automatically drawn in. Their
service period is four months, which seems a lot less than a
year, but it would appear that excellent use is being made of
the lesser period, since Major-General McNaughton, com-
manding all Canadian forces in England, has expressed himself as delighted with the fine state of preparation of the units
which from time to time join his command, and these units
are derived from the four-month draftees, in large part by
voluntary enlistment. Much has been most unjustly said in
the United States by certain parties, who shall be nameless
because each of you can name them so readily, on the fact
that Canada has not adopted conscription. To such statements
there are at least two replies. First, Canada did not adopt conscription in the First World War until three years of war
had passed, and in that struggle the call for man power was
more emphatic than it is now. Second, Canada has a French
population amounting to about 38 per cent of her whole
number of citizens, and they are something less than enthusiastic about this struggle—as they were, on the whole, about
the last. If about 40 per cent of American population situated
en masse in a single section of the country were known to be
cold on the draft, I venture to express a doubt whether the
Selective Service Act could ever have ridden the jumps to

success. So much for the men of the traditional services; when it comes to the air, Canada will perhaps be, after the war, the headquarters for the central air defense of the British Commonwealth, with a personnel, as I have already said, containing in its ranks the best trained military birdmen in the world simply because they will have learned through the hard way of war how to handle the airplane in actual combat. Then, too, the seamen of her rapidly growing navy are learning to challenge the seamen of the Royal Navy in courage, endurance, and resourcefulness, and further than that praise could not go. The German convoy-raiding U-boat has learned to hate the sight of the Canadian corvettes, swift as hawks and as merciless when they have pounced on their prey. Canadian industry, as previously noted, is turning out munitions of war of high quality at a swift tempo, now that the awkwardness of the change-over from peace production has been overcome, and her factories now carry through all stages the construction and boring of huge rifled cannon. Canada is staggering under a bill of expense which for war alone will take one-third of the national income and for all governmental expenses well over 40 per cent. That would mean a comparable expenditure by the United States this year of thirty billion dollars for war purposes and forty billions for all purposes of government. Even with our capacity for reeling off astronomical figures, let us admit that these are pretty tidy sums. A Canadian in my profession at a like stage of academic advancement, married but without dependents, pays now about three times the income tax I shall be called upon to pay here next March. And finally, it is a peculiarly mean slander to say that Canada is charging Great Britain cash on the barrel head while the United States is lending and leasing without reckoning the cost. The truth is that Canada is by herself financing a large part of British purchasing in America, and further one must remember that Canada needed some cash help to transform her peacetime industry to a wartime footing. It is pleasant, then, to be able to report to an American audience that, so far as hemispheric defense is concerned, Canada is doing the great thing in the great way that Americans have learned to expect of her; that is, those Americans who have followed her achievement at all. If the Monroe Doctrine has been a little bent out of shape to cover the unusual status of that American nation which is Canada, Americans can rest assured that there will be none more ready, none more aggressively prepared to see that, however bent the Doctrine may have to be to fit new corners, it will never be broken so far as the people north of the line are concerned. If an American secretary of state could feel as confident of the certainty and the quality of defense of the Monroe Doctrine that some important South American states would put up, he would be able to sleep better of nights. And of course the account I have given of Canada's war effort is sketchy; I have really had eastern Canada largely in mind and I have said nothing about the twenty-five wireless stations which cover Canada's vast northwestern territory under the direction of the Department of National Defense, nor of the landing fields which Canada, in conjunction with the United States, is building surely and steadily on the inner side of the Rockies in order that a plane may never be more than one hundred miles from good landing between the international border and Alaska. On the west coast as on the east, whoever is the enemy of the United States is the enemy of Canada as well. Few Americans know that Great Britain was compelled to denounce her Anglo-Japanese pact in 1921 because the representatives of Canada insisted that the continued existence of that pact threatened the permanence of good relations between the United States and Canada. It may be that Canada cannot decide against the United States, but it may also be true that she does not want to, either.

Now the next consideration beyond this is the planning and administration of hemispheric defense from the viewpoint of its northern end. For the planning of this defense a frank and unfearful exchange of available knowledge as it exists and as it is acquired is essential between the two countries. There should be going on continuously a minute and thorough study by the military and naval men of the two countries of every feature of the terrain of Canada and of the adjoining seas, and there should be proceeding constantly discussions of how attack should be met, no matter through or over what medium it comes, at any and every conceivable point that could be employed for that purpose. Where one of the two countries concerned cannot possibly contemplate aggression on the other, and where the other country is by the will of its citizens committed, despite all its power, actual and potential, to a policy of nonaggression, there should be no silly difficulties created on either side which would impair the value of these joint studies and discussions on the ground that military and naval secrets were being betrayed.

But it is highly essential that if this policy is adopted it should be steadily and seriously worked at, that it should be regarded as of supreme importance and should be administered in that light. For something near a year now there has been, it is true, a joint American-Canadian commission on defense, and for a short time after its formation we learned of its activities by reports of extensive trips it was taking to very interesting spots with good hotels and excellent facilities for entertainment; perhaps they were also of military and naval significance. Of its American members, as I could not speak from knowledge, I shall say nothing, but I am quite certain that Canadians were more amused than impressed by the list of Canadian nominees to the commission when it appeared in the newspapers. That the joint commission is not now functioning cannot, of course, be concluded from the fact that it is no longer mentioned by the press; but that is a purely negative approach, and one would like to know, indeed every citizen of both countries has an interest in knowing, that it is functioning, and functioning usefully, and making every preparation that human foresight and energy can devise against the bringing of Armageddon to American soil through the north, northeast, or northwest Canadian approach. This is one place of all places where an ornamental grouping of political appointees cannot be tolerated; what is needed is a body of hard-bitten men who know what war has been, now is, and is capable of becoming, and who will undertake trips by sea, land, or air to remote and difficult shores where a good French dinner would be a great deal more difficult to get than in San Francisco and a swing orchestra and a floor show a little less likely to be included in the repertoire than in New York or Montreal. It should be insisted from the first that no one should serve on such a commission unless qualified by knowledge, experience, and technical ability to make his weight count. If my auditors will just think of the painstaking way in which a German general staff for the invasion of North America would be set up, composed of first-rate experts fully advised on every possible phase of the undertaking, they will have in mind the sort of joint defense commission I conceive might profitably be established. Surely at this time Americans and Canadians have got it through their rather amiably stupid heads that to the Axis powers, and especially Germany and Japan, war is a business and it is a business in which those have the best likelihood of success who have best prepared themselves to deserve success.

I confess to feeling very uneasy about this joint defense commission. If the Axis powers were going to deliver an assault on America through the territory of Canada, the moment the marshals and generals were named we would recognize them for men of ability and grim experience, capable and ruthless, because they would all be first-class names in military annals; there would be no war-office clerks or arm-chair colonels among them. If it is actually the case that democracies can function only at low potential in such vital matters, carrying into commissions like this, involving life and death even nationally perhaps, those amiable ideas about setting up commissions which prevail under conditions of peace, they are, to put it frankly, going to have a very hard time to survive, and they are going to deserve to have a very hard time; that means, of course, not that some abstraction called democracy is going to have a hard time, but that you and I, our children, our relatives, our friends, our neighbors, are going to have a bad time and that some of them and us are going to be hurt and that some of them and us will be killed. We cannot say of a joint defense commission for the United States and Canada in the matter of hemispheric protection what we usually say about such things: "Oh, it's just another commission set up to still a momentary popular clamor and head off the achievement of any serious or worthwhile result!" It may be that democracies can afford to make ordinary commissions the graveyards of attempts to let a little light into the blackouts of politics and to institute progressive action, but if that is the best they can do with a joint defense commission, as in the case of the United States and Canada, they had better get ready to hang out the "Business for Sale" sign. No embattled farmers are going to get far in a world of tanks, airplanes, and high explosives, and no armchair colonels are going to stop cold, hard-faced men who fight first and drink cocktails afterwards if at all.

In this connection I cannot even begin to understand why in the recent much-publicized meeting on the Atlantic between President Roosevelt and Mr. Churchill no room was found in the ensemble for Premier Mackenzie King of Canada. It is quite possible that Mr. Churchill does not quite trust Mackenzie King because Mr. King has always been North American in his outlook, which no one, I suppose, would maintain that Mr. Churchill is; but Mr. Roosevelt has been Mr. King's personal friend for years, and I should have expected him to urge the latter's inclusion in the discussion group. Indeed, I think it might have been most salutary for the President to have had Mr. King there, because, whatever a Canadian knows or does not know in general, he has great ability in one particular field: he has learned by long and frequently painful experience how to size up an Englishman and to realize by a kind of instinct what he is fishing for in any given argument or discussion. An American is far more likely to be taken in when dealing with a Britisher than a Canadian is, and if I were an American going into conference with a very astute Englishman I would always take a Canadian along to prod me in the ribs whenever the Englishman was getting dangerous. I mention the whole incident in connection with a joint defense commission because it seems to me very important that the United States and all those who represent the authority of the United States should, in every international meet or move involving the defense of the northern half of the Western Hemisphere, either themselves consider or insist that others consider the inclusion of Canada in the discussions and negotiations. Good will is a thing to be cultivated, not just assumed, and one of the best ways of cultivating it has always proved to be the generous recognition of the personality or the nation you are seeking to bind to you in bonds of understanding. If the United States wants to get a tiptop joint defense commission, its way to get it will be to nominate as its delegates men of the very highest rank, ability, and experience, thus indicating that service on this commission is regarded as being of paramount importance. The hint will not be lost on Canada; she will within the range of her possibilities, and, believe me, in the field of war they are not small, name her very best. And when Mr. Roosevelt concludes any pact, if he does so, for the defense of Canada's northeastern coast, he would be well advised to include in it the authorities of Canada as well as those of Britain. If there is to be a land and air defense of Canada, it is Canadians, not Britishers, who will be undertaking it along with Americans, and Mr. Roosevelt ought here to exercise his well-known tact. He should be very careful about the possibility of giving offense here through that lack of thought upon the matter which has characterized so much of America's dealing with Canada, a genuinely American nation which by force of geography must to the end of time itself be the northern neighbor of the United States, unless economic circumstances should convert it, as is always possible, into the northern extension.

The subject allotted to me was "Canada and Hemispheric Defense"; it is really the subject for a volume, and a volume which some competent person should write for a large body of persons to read. In the course of an hour's talk such are the limitations of language that only a few high spots can be touched, and in the selection of these the speaker is no doubt unconsciously influenced by certain biases of his own rather than by any system of rational selection, even though he may flatter himself he is achieving the latter. But I trust that even if you think that there are points I should have touched on which I have omitted, or that I might well have omitted some that I have discussed, or that I should have discussed them in a way different from that in which I chose to handle them, I may have been successful in rousing in you the conviction that Canada is America's problem, preëminently so at the present time under war conditions, but always America's problem, whether in war or in peace. I hope I may have made you resolve to demand of American political and educational leaders that American-Canadian relations be regarded invariably as a subject of first-rate importance both for negotiation and for study. To take any other point of view is to close one's eyes to what should be obvious and would indeed so be if the eyes remained open; it is to become the victim of yet another phase of that wishful thinking which is now so omnipresent with us, with its fatal blight on clear thought and sound action. For the facts are these, plainly and frankly, so far as relates to the United States of America and the year 1941, as expressed by John MacCormac (p. 13), whose brilliant book became a best seller almost immediately after its appearance on the market: "Canada makes isolation impossible for the United States. Canada makes neutrality a fiction. Any day while the present struggle lasts, the United States might be forced to choose between a war over Canada and abandonment of the Monroe Doctrine. The possibility is remote so long as Britain holds her own on land and controls the sea. But it is there."

Canada is an American nation. The aegis of the Monroe Doctrine is spread above her as above every other American nation. It is unthinkable that it should be withdrawn unless America is prepared to step down into the position of a second- or third-rate power. If America is prepared to do that, then all my observations of her people have been erroneous and reflect little credit on myself. Hence the importance for every thinking American of trying to grasp the little-understood relationship between Canada and the nearly always imperfectly understood and often erroneously reported Monroe Doctrine. It is the matter of that relationship that, once comprehended, is sure to lead as directly as a line traced by a perfect straightedge to the question we are here considering—the question of Canada and Hemispheric Defense. If the fact that little has heretofore been said about it does not arise merely from that general know-nothing attitude about Canada which seems to be about the most continuous of all American fashions, it is a great compliment to Canada; it implies a belief that, if this hemisphere is going to need defense, Canada is one place where Uncle Sam will not have to do all the defending. And those places will not be too numerous.

AIR POWER FOR THE DEFENSE
OF THE AMERICAS

———

BALDWIN M. WOODS
PROFESSOR OF MECHANICAL ENGINEERING
IN THE UNIVERSITY OF CALIFORNIA

Lecture delivered October 8, 1941

AIR POWER FOR THE DEFENSE
OF THE AMERICAS

TODAY—not a few years from now—designers and manufacturers know enough to build airplanes for nearly any purpose, of sizes adequate to meet most needs, and of excellent operating characteristics. But an understanding of the uses for them lags badly.

The growth of cities affords an easy illustration of the problem. Up to 1900, the cities of the world developed to a radius which would permit a man living at the circumference to walk to work near the center of town. The horse played a small role and permitted those with horse and buggy to live a little farther out. The suburban train was coming into use for mass transportation in a few centers. The electric street car did not become a material factor until after 1900.

By 1910 the automobile began to influence conditions appreciably. The city's radius grew more rapidly. It is now twenty miles or more. The time by automobile rather than the distance determines the radius. Moreover, the degree of adjustment of the city to the automobile determines the kind of transformation that takes place in the area. Congested transportation leads to distributed shopping and business centers, to the decay of downtown districts. Wholly inadequate provision of parking space and of street-traffic capacities has delayed normal adjustment and has caused disruption. Important lessons have been learned which will permit better solutions for the future. Parking-space needs can now be computed and plans be made accordingly. Needless to say, skyscrapers for workers who drive automobiles call for sky-scrapers for their cars of much the same size. Also, intersect-ing highways forming grids lose capacity in cars per hour, depending upon the number of intersections. Confusion is worse confounded. Four-lane highways suffer a greater per-centage loss from intersections than two-lane streets. The traffic problem of today is fundamentally a city problem. Interstate highways outside of highly populous areas are much simpler. Naturally, solutions are costly and most cities face a compromise between rebuilding the center and per-mitting development of competing units on the periphery. The adjustment is certainly not more than half accomplished. The present achievements have been acquired too slowly and at great expense. They are: an understanding of the problem, and a method of reducing it to a scientific or design basis. Most of the actual work is still to be done.

By 1930 the airplane was recognized as a normal mode of transport. Today it carries in the United States a substantial proportion of the long-haul luxury passenger traffic. The air-plane as a vehicle of transport for the owner-pilot is coming. Within the past five years the annual production of light air-planes for owner operation in this country has risen from about 100 to more than 6000. William B. Stout, a leader in this field, forecasts 100,000 or more per year, as soon as defense demands for materials and labor are sufficiently relaxed. What will this mean to the cities? Many potential effects cannot be foreseen, but a strong decentralizing influence appears certain. Stout prophesies a city radius of 75 to 100 miles. Clearly the fixed boundary between city and country is to go, like the fixed battle line and fixed defense line. To visualize the possibilities of combined automobile and airplane traffic and the services these can render to civilization is a challenge which confronts America—a challenge also faced by the rest of the world.

The problem pictured here is one of peace conditions, although the effects are quite revolutionary. The automobile is attacking the city's business center today just about as effectively as army bombers. No new inventions, radical improvements, or special laws are necessary for the effects of the airplane to follow a course like those of the automobile. Moreover, research brings advances faster now than ever before and many inventions will be made. Over 50,000 per year are now patented. But it isn't necessary to assume these in order to recognize the problems of the city and the need for flexible designs and plans for its future. The airplane will surely augment the already powerful influences of the automobile.

In the field of warfare, the automobile and the airplane are also major influences in the changes of the past twenty years. If the radio is added, which serves both automobile and airplane, progress in equipment for warfare appears to consist in developing instruments already available in the present world war. It is the extent of utilization and the number of uses which show imagination and willingness to face change.

The tank is the automobile, fort, and field gun in one. The bomber is the 600-mile Big Bertha, perhaps the 6000-mile gun of tomorrow. For these to be effective the service and communication lines must be similarly stretched and accelerated.

Mechanized industry in turn must supply its streams of supplies. Food, equipment, and munitions must flow to the points of need as fast and as certainly as they are used. The transportation problem is fundamental. One of the most credible stories of the war in Russia in 1941 is that the orders for the German attack and advance into Russia were not given until after a last conference between the high command and the transportation chiefs.

The transport lines are like fire hoses. The flow through them must be adequate to put out the fire in spite of length or size of the hoses. Warfare now demands much longer range of action than it did and much greater consumption of munitions for each unit operating. If the range is doubled and the quantity of material used is also doubled, the ton-miles of transportation rise at least fourfold. Bottlenecks become more serious. The capacity of a highway or a railway line may become a deciding factor in a campaign. The race to excel in military striking strength is a race to deliver whatever is needed at a given place at a given time.

This is a brief account of the problem of the city and the automobile, and of the army and its motor equipment. What does it indicate? Why is it necessary to a discussion of air defense? It indicates, first, that transportation of goods and men is a strenuous and vital problem; and second, that imagination about possible extensions and variations of present uses is equally vital.

What is sounder than to adapt available equipment to new uses, when simple changes will make the present trucks, tanks, guns, or airplanes do the job? Further, this account is necessary to a discussion of air defense because the airplane is doing to the combat area what the automobile is doing to the city. Also, like the automobile, its ability to carry something besides its own weight makes it capable of providing answers to transportation problems as yet unsolved. The airplane is now carrying troops and equipment. It stands today, with reference to warfare, where the automobile stood in 1918.

As aerial forms of the airplane are developed comparable to the ground forms of the automobile, the resulting changes in the nature of warfare can be imagined. Also, the fact that the air has numerous possible traffic lanes between any two points provides excellent air-lane capacity. The airplane will develop along these lines and others, as all students recognize. The problem of defense will be determined by who sees first what can be done and does it.

What, then, is the best approach to the problem of the air defense of the Americas? It is the well-known method of the military engineer. Assume the enemy to have superior brains, men, and equipment—to be supermen, in fact—and design the defense accordingly. As an example, assume that they can put any needed force in the field by air, that they can adequately equip it, and provide the necessary munitions and supplies, all by air. In other words, assume that the hostile power uses imagination and skill to get the limit in transportation by air. Assume also that it uses for every transportation or other purpose the equipment which will give the most in speed, capacity, and range: airplanes, tanks, motorized supply trains. Also, assume the key attack to be made where it is difficult to oppose, say somewhere south of the equator.

The problem is propounded in this form, not because an attack can or cannot be made now in this way, but because it is the obvious way to try. Every few months, one hears of new military uses of aircraft. The parachute troops, intended to overcome inability to land at hostile airports, are one example. Trains of gliders to increase man-carrying capacity of airplanes and to furnish low-speed machines such as gliders for rough landings or for landing on water are another. Equally important, but less spectacular, are the fleets of airplanes designed for freight carrying. The next problem for any air force is to develop all these services into a military pattern of maximum effectiveness. This is the obvious trend of today.

One of the principles of engineering often overlooked by the critics is the necessity of doing every job with available tools and materials. The young designer wants special sizes of steel or duralumin bars and tubes. If he insists, he must often wait until they are made for him—sometimes after many months. A machine of slightly less perfect design, based on sizes and shapes which are in stock near at hand, would be finished long before the new parts alone can be delivered. Some contractors for defense munitions have started production months ahead of their associates simply by taking available machine tools, even used ones, and altering them to serve the purpose. This amounts to increasing the nation's machine-tool production for the time involved.

Likewise, the air system of the Americas must be built from what we have. There is a tendency to overrate a new special-purpose military plane and to undervalue all the other parts of the system. The military authorities, aided by continual receipt of information concerning other forces, must ultimately decide the character and number of military planes of the types needed. With the aid of governmental laboratories, conceded to rank among the best in the world, performance of airplanes must be at the best. With the strengthening both of coördination of all arms of national defense and of the capabilities of the special services, difficult problems of efficiency must be solved. It is not necessary to attempt here to appraise the quality of American pursuit, attack, bombing, and general-purpose planes to appreciate the magnitude of the air-defense problem. Army, navy, and constructing designers will continue to do two jobs simultaneously, build rapidly planes already designed, and design new ones of superior characteristics. There is ample evidence that this is being done. The current criticism of some types of pursuit and bombing planes is undoubtedly beneficial in keeping designers alert; it may be damaging if it seriously weakens public confidence in the arms of national defense. During the years of small appropriations for army and navy development, it was apparent that no considerable numbers of airplanes could be built. Therefore, appropriations were wisely divided between development of new types and limited construction of current ones. As a result, it was necessary to go through a period of a year or more of factory building and test flying before defense production reached large quantities. This means, however, that a number of plane types now going into production may be expected to excel any produced elsewhere. This is true of fighter planes, as it has long been true of long-distance bombers. The Air Corps reports, for example, that there are only two fighters in the world with speeds substantially over 400 miles per hour and that both are American planes, the Lockheed P-38 and the Republic P-47. Also, American long-range bombers at altitudes of more than 30,000 feet are outclimbing opponents' pursuit planes. Since fast climbing is a specialty of pursuit ships this is a tribute to the supercharger performance of the motors and to the aerodynamic qualities of the ship.

It is important to recognize the enormous administrative and organizational problems both of the Air Corps and the industry during the past sixteen to twenty months. With a general expansion of the Army of 1500 to 2000 per cent and a production-program increase for airplanes of nearly half that much, there were great difficulties. Men of suitable training were far too few. An officer who is highly competent in administering an air station and a unit of men and equipment may or may not be equal to a task ten times as complicated. The jobs were there and men had to be assigned to them. Many changes in assignments have been made, and more will be necessary to get the smooth efficiency which must come.

In the airplane industry the situation is phenomenal. It is a young man's industry. In the largest factories, the organization had developed sufficiently to build two or three hundred planes a year. Thousands were suddenly required. Methods of production must be vitally changed and staffs be trebled and then trebled again. Presidents of the companies were perhaps forty-five years of age, production managers thirty-five, project engineers in charge of designs of critical new airplanes thirty years of age. One who had been with a company more than five years was a patriarch! Only a state of national anxiety can explain discontent with over-all achievements to date. Probably the youth of the management accounts for the amazing speed with which expansion has occurred. It is significant that the young men who build airplanes are among the most serious critics of their own achievements, the most concerned that the production shall not merely be excellent, but that it shall be adequate for the nation's needs. So much energy has been necessary to handle factory reconstruction, employment of personnel, change of design and production procedures, that many important things have lagged. Whatever further increase is necessary, it is likely to be less in degree than growth already achieved. Better planes in large numbers, with much reduction of waste in materials and labor, are to be expected.

Many flyers and others have urged the creation of a separate arm of defense for development and administration of the air service. Doubtless, the correct decision for this question is important. However, the most urgent policy questions must be faced irrespective of whether there is a distinct air-warfare administration or one which operates as part of the existing arms. These questions include: coördination of all arms of national defense, and stimulus and imagination in the development of all major implements. The San Francisco–Oakland Bay Bridge required for its construction the services of engineers who were experts in different fields; civil, geological, mining, electrical, mechanical, for example. The general plan was administered by a board of civil engineers. But the electrical engineers designed a special radio communication system which proved of great value, when isolated pier construction was under way. Likewise, defense or offense must have a coordinated command and an integrated planning agency to utilize the services of every separate service. Further, each service must be developed to its greatest usefulness and must be not merely permitted but urged so to develop. The central planning agency may be expected with reason to have higher goals of achievement for the tank divisions, the naval scouting force, the air service, and so on, than the individual services for themselves. If this should fail to be the case, the nation will lack real defense—the kind which demands the utmost of every agency, combined to give the most powerful result. The most urgent problems appear to be military planning, development, and coördinated administration for the whole national defense. It is likely that the machinery for administrative management can be designed and developed to do this job as well as corresponding organization for building tanks and airplanes is being perfected. Are there not experts in management who can advise wisely on this subject? Are they perhaps already at work upon it?

It was suggested earlier that any plans for air defense should assume that the enemy has as good brains and equipment as we have and that he has devised a plan that will use air transportation and airplane warfare to the limit. Imagination and ingenuity are assumed. It was also suggested that defense must contemplate doing something better. To make the case concrete, assume the necessity of transporting an army with all necessary equipment to any designated area of Central America, South America, Canada, or Alaska, all by air, and the further need for maintaining it there by air. Almost certainly, this cannot now be done by any country. It may not be possible for some time. If, however, it can be done, America should be the first to know how and be best prepared to do the job.

Total war or total defense, as far as air warfare is concerned, means dependence on the sum of all air facilities. Every airplane must land and refuel. The longer the distance between fuel stops, the less it can carry as useful load. Hence, the grid of airports over all the area to be covered is of maximum importance. Moreover, the airports must fit the planes. Either the slower-speed plane must be used or the landing strips increased in length, when the two don't match. The errors of civil and military aviation are like those of all engineering. They come in the simple things. Not enough common radio instruments to equip the planes is far more tragic than failure to get a perfect radio. No airport at all where planes should concentrate is more critical than a long debate on concrete versus macadam runways. A fair to good blind landing system actually installed at every airport where need is great requires no argument against delay while research labors over perfecting the ideal system. This is not to disparage research. The excellence of American equipment today is the direct result of twenty-five years of competent governmental research alone. But production is the twin brother of research. Refinement follows. Also, applied research and construction needs hundreds of engineers to every physicist or chemist who studies the life history of electrons and atoms or the aerodynamics of the boundary layer.

A dozen Edisons and a hundred Fords must accompany every Faraday. The greatest aid to mechanized civilization is applied research. But its widespread use comes too slowly. That use must be speeded or the United States will not be first in the air or on the ground. The public does not know how hard it is to make an invention work, how many steps there are between the gyroscope of the physicist and the gyro-pilot of the engineer. The application of the common inventions to the air defense of America, the engineering of aviation, must move and move fast.

Consider further the airport problem. By the summer of 1940 the airports were scarcely adequate for the traffic. La Guardia Airport handled about 2000 plane arrivals and departures per week—one every five minutes. This is approximately its capacity. In instrument-approach weather there is an overload. The Department of Commerce program, for which initial appropriations were made in 1940, calls for increasing the number of first-class airports from 36 to 500 and medium-sized ones from 245 to 1600. These are in the United States alone. Alaska, Hawaii, Canada, Central America, and South America are confronted by corresponding problems.

The airport with good radio and lighting facilities which can handle an arrival or departure every five minutes is still the exception. Assume 100 movements per hour! If the airport is primarily a refueling stop—all airports are just this in some degree—then gas storage becomes a problem. A transport plane consumes about 100 gallons per hour. It is not uncommon to have refueling on long flights of 500 gallons per plane. If an airport has storage for 25,000 gallons—enough for fifty planes—it has been considered well supplied. For mass movements of the future, storage must go up, fuel-carrying planes must accompany expeditions, or quick means of refueling the airport itself must be at hand.

For bad weather especially, radio aids, including instrument-approach and blind-landing facilities, are required. Full equipment is not so important at little-used airports. For those which must take heavy loads, especially where low clouds and fog are common, failure to provide is serious.

Then there is the question of number and length of runways. As speeds of airplanes have risen, the gliding angle or slope of the airplane path approaching or leaving the airport has flattened. Some years ago, a drop of one foot in seven was used. Now, one in forty is discussed. The take-off run must go up with higher landing speeds. These higher landing speeds are allowed because the cruising speed of the plane can be increased by raising the landing speed. Military planes with 75 to 90 miles per hour landing speeds are here. Commercial planes have moved up, year by year, as they could get airports with longer runways. The result is the demand for large airports—7000-foot runways are commonly mentioned—and large areas of low structures and flat ground configuration around the airport in order to clear planes on a flat flight path. A compromise is indicated. Particularly in countries like Alaska, Central America, and some parts of South America there is no high-speed surface transportation in competition. Except for a few airports to handle long-distance through planes, airports and planes could be harmonized at lower landing speeds. Also, the bigger freight planes of the future can be a little more deliberate in landing, to permit smaller shock loads to the runways. Recent heavy planes break through runway surfaces, especially in bad weather. The airport must be had. Not every airport can handle every plane in all kinds of weather and at any rate desired. Most careful compromises to give the best total result are needed. All the intelligence, imagination, and man power available will not be too much to use.

It is noteworthy that air networks are developing rapidly where railways and highways are lacking or inadequate. Alaska, Central America, and Colombia are striking examples. The airplane at even 100 miles an hour can cover distances in a few hours which require days or weeks by other modes of travel. Costs for passengers or freight are less by air. Traffic develops and communities grow where neither would develop otherwise. In such places, freight by air is an immediate need. Pioneering in moving heavy equipment by airplane is under way in these countries. The competition is not between airplane at 30 to 40 cents per ton-mile and first-class railway at 1 or 2 cents. The airplane cost may be about as stated; the alternative is often several times the cost by air. When national security is involved, cost is not the deciding factor. Valuable time can be saved and advantages be secured by speed.

Generally, development of freight service by air has lagged more in the United States than in some other countries. This is a tribute to the excellence and low cost of rail, highway, and water transport. If low cost were the only basis for selecting air transportation, and if all countries had excellent ground transportation, the future of air freight would be seriously limited. But speed and military competition both demand air shipment of goods. Railways and highways often stop at the border, while the air goes on. With present knowledge, air freight transport is apparently possible at 20 cents or less per ton-mile. To do the job well, special planes will be designed and built. They may be a little slower than passenger planes, have somewhat less expensive navigation equipment and finish, and have bodies designed for quick, easy loading and slow landing. Since a good deal of the traffic will be to less accessible places, freight planes must be prepared for rough landings, muddy airports, and short runways. What a single plane lacks in carrying capacity, it often supplies through frequency of its trips. The transport freighter will operate to extend other transport. A body designed to carry a loaded truck provides a mode of transport beyond its landing place. Such possibilities are numerous. They challenge the imagination.

Many more examples of the simple things out of which the greatest air system will be built could be mentioned. The result will come from the use of what lies at hand. Awaiting the new principle or new invention is to miss the very process which will bring it. Anyone can state the parts of the problem. Likewise, the baffled housewife, driving downtown on a shopping tour, can state the city's traffic problem and its solution: enough parking space for all the cars and enough streets without intersections to carry the traffic! What is simpler? The fact is that the city will have no solution if the attempted ones ignore the very difficulties mentioned.

So, a program of air defense will include the airports, planes, and facilities mentioned. Some of the chief aims will be:

1) A general one. To provide adequate force for defense at any needed point. To attempt air transport of everything required. To accept limitations where greater efficiency is thereby obtained or where present development of aircraft is inadequate.

2) Particular aims.

a) To develop domestic airlines and airports as the foundation of an air defense, as the laboratory for development, and as a national transportation service. Subject them to capacity and endurance tests.

b) To build planes for tomorrow. Some will be freakish designs for peculiar purposes. There will be freighters designed as such, not converted passenger planes. Also, some will be bigger planes, clearly exploratory in character, intended for the greatest distances and the heaviest loads. Included will be the flivver planes for the commuter or suburban dweller. All are important.

c) To install and operate strategic lines. These will cover the hemisphere, as they are rapidly doing. They will go to any place to which it is important to maintain access. This may mean everywhere.

3) To obtain coördination.

a) Military, commercial, and sport flying must serve one another. When total defense is paramount, its needs must dictate activities.

b) Planning must include the whole of the air effort. Specifically, it must seek four things, as follows.

Common understanding of the problem.

Public awareness that expensive developments outside the United States are involved.

Integration of uses of airways, airports, and airplanes.

Maximum use of local initiative but sufficient central authority to insure success.

Whatever air defense is obtained will be developed from what there is. Every effort to obtain the best direction for building the force will presumably be exerted. If the talent for execution is at hand—and who doubts that it is?—planes, airports, and organization will evolve. Tremendous effort and initiative have marked the growth of army, navy, air transport, and manufacturing agencies during the past year or more. The questions raised here are some of those which everyone needs to know about in order to understand what is being attempted.

Once again, imagination and initiative are the priceless attributes of air-defense executives. A great psychiatrist recently discussed the slow adjustment of man to "action at a distance." "Perhaps a hundred thousand years were necessary," he said, "for man to adjust himself to the change which came when he learned to throw a stone for a purpose." Action at arm's length prescribed one world, action at a stone's throw a larger, more complex one. Civilization makes a long stone's throw with its airplanes. Tragic as present war uses are, they may stimulate imagination and initiative enough to make the airplane the greatest aid to international understanding yet developed. This is, as Stevenson said, "a task for all that a man has of fortitude and delicacy."

WHITHER PAN-AMERICANISM?

HERBERT I. PRIESTLEY
PROFESSOR OF MEXICAN HISTORY
IN THE UNIVERSITY OF CALIFORNIA
AND DIRECTOR OF THE BANCROFT LIBRARY

Lecture delivered October 15, 1941

WHITHER PAN-AMERICANISM?

THERE EXISTS in our country today, I fear, a large degree of indifference toward the real meaning of our Latin-American relations and of Latin-American attitudes toward the world revolution. Some people feel that our southern neighbors live in a semicultivated state, raising raw products too profusely to find consumers; that they are mostly "natives" in the deprecatory sense of the word; that they are viciously pro-German and hostile to ourselves, but that a quick landing of our marines in any disturbed area would apply the needed touch of assurance. Those who feel so would now have a more realistic conception of the Pan-American situation if the uprising of Nazis last year in Uruguay had not been put down by the Uruguayans; if President Ávila Camacho in Mexico were as pro-German as was Carranza in World War I; if Vargas in Brazil were really as hostile to democracy as he once sounded; if Ambassador von Thermann in Argentina were to carry pro-Nazi elements in that country with him in his schemes to add that country to the Axis realm.

These are the short-term considerations of national defense growing out of the current emergency. The longer-term values of cultural affinity are being slowly built up; if we persevere we shall not long hence find out that our southern neighbors have scientists, writers, and educators of parts, just as we have in a small way learned that they have archaeologists, painters, and musicians of great ability and mentality. When the preoccupations of colonialism and imperialism have been superseded by appreciation for the artistic and scientific value of each of the three peoples concerned, we shall come into mutual respect for the mentality and the true worth of our so-called Latin-American and Anglo-Saxon cultures, making our intellectual neighborliness as dignified and stable as our former contacts with Europe.

When Pan-Americanism was first conceived it was for the purpose of uniting the Spanish American countries in a sort of defensive alliance to ward off reconquest by the mother country. There was to be also mutuality of cultural relations beneath treaty relations of political import. Only as a second thought was the United States included in the design, and our participation was fruitless in the first congress. After that one at Panama, the emphasis for a long time was upon Hispanism, that is, as the idea of union grew, it was directed as much or more against the United States as against the home countries. Very little actual accomplishment grew out of those early conferences, except the habit of trying to unite. After many failures, by the last quarter of the nineteenth century the idea of continental union had developed into an attempt to create an American sphere for the neomercantilism of the epoch. On the part of the United States, the idea of James G. Blaine grew into an effort to assert and preserve the hegemony of this nation in the trade of the Americas and in those international political relations which are considered purely continental. Culture was talked of, but not very seriously taken.

Since the new states had chosen the form of republics, their effort was to prevent the encroachment of monarchies, whether by colonization, diplomacy, or war, upon the lives of the western nations. It was to a degree a multiple expression of the declaration of the United States in the Monroe Doctrine. It was a defensive mechanism approaching as closely as might be to that declaration of the French Revolution which described itself as "a war of all peoples against all kings," or, more properly speaking, a defense of all republics against all European monarchies. French help to the British colonies in 1778 had been for vengeance because of imperial losses by France in 1763, so that the wars of the eighteenth century continued the growth of the modern imperial process as forerunners of World Wars I and II, exhibiting the spirit of capitalism and imperialism, which is today being pushed to the *reductio ad absurdum* since it has become physically possible for Germany to obliterate a rival, not merely to conquer him.

By the time the people of the United States had occupied the breadth of the continent, the resurgence of neomercantilism moved us into Cuba, and we joined in emulating the policies of the imperialist states of Europe in the race for empire. No doubt the worst possible characteristic of the present war is the obvious purpose of all the powers concerned to continue the policies which caused all the earlier colonial or imperial wars, with as yet ill-formed plans to relieve the historical process of its destructive attributes of international jealousy.

The inconclusive war of 1914–1918 brought Germany to shame and prostration, but as she recuperated her strength she came to the ideal of dominion over all German-speaking peoples, then to the mastery of Europe, of Asia, and of Africa. Now she wants to rule the whole world, reducing the nations to various congeries of satrapies.

The United States, observing the threat, knew that the realization of the Hitler dream would in time isolate our country and turn our neighboring republics into dictatorships dependent economically and politically upon a German-dominated Europe. Our natural reaction was to try "Continental Solidarity" as an intensification of Pan-Americanism. Almost immediately the role of this country became that of a qualified ally of Great Britain and France; we became champions of a "way of life" called democracy, and sought in hemispherical unity the removal of the threat of propaganda or subversion to the institutions of a Germanized Europe. When, as the war progressed, the United States became successively the arsenal, larder, and treasury for most if not all the nations which resist German aggressions, we had a defensive setup, of which Pan-Americanism is an essential part; it is, like the Monroe Doctrine, a precautionary measure for our own benefit. While its trend will depend largely upon the course of events within the various American countries, its success will in far greater degree depend upon solution of those vaster issues which now preoccupy the world. If there is a German victory there certainly will be no Pan-Americanism, or indeed few of our other aspirations and faiths. If the Allies win, the fate of Pan-Americanism may still be in the balance.

It was the sudden swiftness of the German successes in western Europe which caused the United States to breathe new purpose into Pan-Americanism as a defense to our vicinity from the European whirlwind. There followed a flood of efforts to discover economic and political safety in hemispheric conferences, more reciprocity treaties, proposed cartels, and other controls over commerce. More actively came the conscription of men, appropriations, and measures to create adequate defenses, the Lease-Lend Act, review of defaulted loans and grants of new ones for defense of the Americas, crowding heel upon heel, until we now have obligated ourselves for some fifty-three billions of dollars for "defense" while we have troops on faraway islands not previously considered of moment, and our navy is "shooting at sight" in the Atlantic, and our Neutrality Act is in for a revision toward the side of belligerency.

In the economic sphere of continental collaboration we have met with several successes, but we have found, as Professor Condliffe pointed out in the first lecture of this series, that no cartel, nor continental monopoly, nor self-sufficiency can be maintained between Latin America and ourselves, because of the long dependence of South America upon the European market and trade as a condition of prosperous commerce. Regional controls will prove ineffective, even destructive, because our export of United States manufactures for South American raw products does not equal the available production. The prospect is, moreover, that increasing industrialization of South America will decrease our manufacturing export, and of its own self cause greater raw production in South America. A real world trade is essential to rational and profitable movement of goods and exchange.

In the political sphere the Latin countries are, so far as the party in control in each is concerned, almost unanimous in professed allegiance to the principles of the free way of life; yet, as Professor Fitzgibbon told us in the second lecture, the

Nazi infiltration is widespread and ominous in most of the Latin-American countries. Although some open and other secret risings have been put down, new ones may occur. If the attempt in Uruguay had been successful in 1940, the entire South American waterway system of communications would have been laid open to the spread of Nazi disorders and defections. Buenos Aires is a seat of Nazi influence, and there are minority parties and military cliques in practically all the countries, ready to seize upon the moment of confusion to which many of those governments are susceptible. Since the party in power in most of the Latin-American nations is a one-man party or a coalition government with a meager majority, and since the tenet of the opposition is usually hostile to that of the existing setup, the danger of a political reversal is rarely absent, and some exercise of influence by the United States likely to be asked for. This is one of the main purposes of Nazi troublemaking, from Mexico southward. The engagement of any United States forces upon any Latin-American soil would be extremely hazardous, and is to be avoided at great cost. The defection of a single Latin-American state would be the signal for wider spread, and United States aid to one country alone could very seriously hamper our coöperation with European enemies of Hitler at any critical moment.

Such a contingency, Professor Alexander pointed out in the third lecture, is not likely to arise in our relations with Canada. While the danger of invasion of that country by air forces may be perhaps more likely than invasion of Latin America, the resistance of the populace will presumably be more effective, as Canada is actually at war and has numerous forces available. The Canadians have, moreover, shown inclination to coöperate in the maintenance of military and diplomatic continental contacts by exchanging ministers with several of the southern countries.

Last week, Professor Woods told us how our present air defenses are growing toward prevention of German air invasion; and he implied that the way to obviate attack is to demonstrate air superiority beforehand. At the same time, the growth of enemy air power, as rehearsed and prophesied by Major Seversky, a reputable air expert, writing in the October *Atlantic,* makes evident that air competition is the key to the continuing race for victory. A thousand superbombers, not yet created but in prospect within five years, could make whole nations their targets, resulting in unimaginable destruction, against which naval defense is problematical. By our scientific skill we are widening the diameter of the earth, diabolism making it even larger in diameter than the Creation did, but leaving it an impossible home for man unless he has supremacy in the substratosphere. The only way to escape catastrophe is to destroy the other fellow first. Possibly preparation to do just that may weaken his will to try the hazard.

Fortunately our naval needs have long been foreseen by our President, who has been increasing our forces on the seas since 1933; though, if we accept the dictum of Major Seversky, naval armament without air supremacy is futile, and we must come to depend upon giant bombers in swarms, costing enough to build many battleships. The President may be more sea-minded than air-minded, yet he has long seen this war as cataclysmic, as his actions prove. His challenge to Hitler has been forthright, and often in advance of the demands of clear-sighted supporters. Some of this prevision we may discern in the early bills for the increase of our navy, the trade of destroyers for the air and sea ports in British America, in his successes in getting air bases in Latin America, in allowing use of our ports to repair British ships, in the training of British airmen on our flying fields, in rapid aid to the enemies of Hitler, his determination to see our Lease-Lend goods delivered in Britain and elsewhere, the "shoot at sight" orders to the navy, and in the current moves to restore our neutrality policy to its normal status in international law.

Assistance has been given by frequent loans to China, by attempts to help unfortunate Greece, to aid the government-in-exile of Poland, to supply Russia with matériel of war, efforts to reform the desperate finances of many Latin-American states in spite of, or in efforts to recuperate, our decade-old losses in many of them. Finally, in his frequent declarations of purpose to end Hitler and Hitlerism, Roosevelt has given us the leadership of a man who is "bold, resolute, and inflexible; whose roots are buried deep in American soil; whose blood is American blood, and whose hopes, desires, ideals, and dreams are of and with and for America."

The critics of the President have accused him of many insincerities, among them that of getting us involved by indirection in "another old imperial war." True, the aims of the British are to defend an empire, but it is an empire in which the emphasis has been for years upon improvement of retarded peoples, an empire which has found for its own

Dominions an independence and self-respect which makes them defenders of all their members in this crisis. It is a war, furthermore, which promises, in the terms of its Atlantic Charter, to assure the disarming of Germany and the policing of the ocean ways to prevent repetition of this atrocious preoccupation with unique dominion. On the other side it is an imperial war in which the German sets himself above the rest of mankind, attempting to create a dominion blatantly promising to reduce the world to slavery, as it is doing in the conquered countries of Europe today, mowing down thousands of helpless victims lacking arms for self-defense but refusing to accept the blight put upon them.

The cause of humanity, let alone the commitments of the United States, expects the hearty, self-interested coöperation of the Latin-American nations in support of the will to victory over this modern diabolism. That they do so coöperate is shown by many acts, as already stated, and by their performance in this present financial crisis—vastly better than their resistance to the depression of 1931, when nearly a dozen changes in government followed bankruptcy in the hope of some form of fiscal and financial recovery. The Nazis have as yet failed to bring about defection in Uruguay, Brazil, Argentina, or Chile, where disorders have threatened. The fighting in the northwest, between Ecuador and Peru, has not spread, and by careful measures may be prevented from doing so. There has been a good response to the measures of the State Department in exchanges of visitors who make for understanding, and especially to the recent energetic work of Vice-President Wallace's Economic Defense Board. This agency has moved with new determination to help the South American countries rebuild their foreign trade, which has been tragically hurt by the removal of German, Italian, and Japanese markets. The work of the new board ends a bottleneck hampering export, and review of previously refused licenses will make for rapid movement of some $170,000,000 worth of goods. It may be remarked in passing that not only his energy, but his command of Spanish and his genial disposition, are making Wallace's name one to conjure with in Spanish America. This has been already demonstrated in the case of Mexico, where the visit of the Vice-President did much to relieve the long-drawn-out tension between our country's oil companies and the Mexican government. If we had been at loggerheads with Mexico at the outbreak of the present war, we might have experienced such troubles as we saw during the time of Carranza in the First World War. The heartening grant of air bases in Mexico saves us from fear of air invasions from our southern border, whereas it is still possible to work out the problem of debts and expropriations without creating any breach in the coöperation of the two countries on the question of continental defense. The difficulties of Bolivia and Standard Oil, while not so deep as those of the oil companies in Mexico, have not prevented our arrangements for obtaining tungsten and tin, upon which our effort depends. We need yet a high official who can travel on his Portuguese.

The countries of Latin America seek coöperation and coördination with the United States; if for nothing else, because we are the nearest great power. But it must be confessed that several of their governments are living on borrowed time, with markets destroyed and their business stagnant. Their scant resources must be used to full capacity, and their loyalty must be measured by the assistance we give them and the prestige we maintain in a hideous world. This means that their governments friendly to us must be maintained in power in spite of surprises, and their self-interest joined to our own in every practical way possible.

Perhaps a survey of some of the internal troubles of the Latin-American states will convey an idea of how hard the maintenance of a solid front against the vicious menace from Europe can be. In the Argentine, for instance, Nazism has been led by the German ambassador, Edmund von Thermann. The Radical Party would gladly expel him, and the Damonte Taborda Anti-Nazi Committee of the Argentine congress has forced resolutions against him, but the acting president, Castillo, fears to encourage such action. Taborda is also after various blind Nazi organizations. The country, bereft of its president because of illness, still suffers from corrupt provincial elections, and the hostility of the senate to the party in power in the chamber of deputies. It may be feared that the Nazi group will take advantage of the political disorganization to seize power. If the Argentine should join its interests with the Nazis, the southern continent would be the seat of great danger. The recent campaign of press attacks and insults by the Nazis because of the actions of the chamber against their "social and charitable clubs" and their chamber of commerce follows the oft-repeated European pattern, indicating a fear-pressure movement which might boomerang.

The conservative Argentine senate refused to follow the attitude of the deputies, and the congress adjourned, leaving a large United States loan unnegotiated, and provincial elections unprotected by national laws against corrupt practices.

The attitude of Brazil has somewhat improved since President Vargas, upon the recent anniversary of Brazilian independence, spoke in complimentary words of Pan-Americanism, in sharp contrast with his wider-heralded speech of June, 1940, in which he praised "virile peoples in search of their destiny" in the style of the once rampageous Mussolini. Contrary to general opinion, the United States bumble-puppied its diplomatic relations with Brazil through most of our history until the presidency of Franklin Delano Roosevelt. What we might once have done would have been to make special treaties with Argentina, Brazil, Chile, and Mexico. In Brazil, as in Portugal, the report persists after several denials that Brazil—and no other power—will be allowed (by Portugal) to take over the Azores in case the Nazis overrun Spain and Portugal. Possibly Brazil could hold the islands, and her tenure would relieve the United States of some onus; but Brazilian naval power would have to be reinforced before use of the islands for defense or offense would be effective. It may be remarked in passing that the Brazilian financial position has recently been much improved by the raising of coffee quotas and prices—at the expense of coffee drinkers in this country. Brazil feels that prices of United States goods are too high, and our ascending spiral of prices may work harm there and in several other low-exchange Latin countries.

The work of squeezing out all Nazi air companies proceeds.

Two lines, Lati and Condor, have been blacklisted, and are being absorbed by Pan Air do Brasil. The Sedta line is out of Ecuador, and Scadta out of Colombia, but there are still German airlines over Brazil, Uruguay, Argentina, and Chile. Their menace would be obvious in case of air invasion from Europe.

A curious turn in the Chilean domestic situation occurred when the war in Russia began, when the Socialists, who had split with the Communists, withdrew their charge that the Communists were "traitors." These two parties, with the Radicals, compose the "Popular Front," and they have been working together with the Chilean president, whose Radicalism is of the variety of Republicanism in the United States. After six Radical cabinet members left office, the last one, then refusing to resign, recently passed from power, but the nonpolitical substitutes ask for restoration of the resigned Radicals. More important is the tension with Germany over arrest of thirty Nazi ringleaders, and the reciprocal arrest by Germany of nine Chileans in Europe for "subversive activities." This spilling over of Nazi animosity into Chile may prove a boomerang, even in a country where the old settlers are Germanic to a degree.

The internal situation of Colombia continues disturbed, as was seen recently when certain Liberals and a Conservative minority walked out of the senate in protest against the candidacy of President López for return to power in 1942. He is said to favor a "collective system" of society. The Conservative Party leader is hostile to the United States.

Peru keeps invading Ecuador, rejecting mediation by the

United States, Argentina, and Brazil. She also rebuffed a Mexican proffer. Costa Rica has expelled all German officials, because the Germans closed Costa Rican consulates in occupied Europe. In Uruguay anti-Nazi proclivities are still shown by contacts with the Argentine Damonte Taborda Anti-Nazi Committee, and by suspension for two weeks of the pro-Nazi paper *El Pampero* for printing an allegation that the "United States is trying to conquer South America with dollars."

A new party in Ecuador, UNE—Unión Nacional Ecuatoriana—has been organized with distinguished members (not Conservatives) who refuse to oust their disliked president during the crisis with Peru. This party favors the United States.

In Mexico trends toward strife are noticed. From that country have gone four delegates, with free rides to Spain furnished by General Franco, to attend a Pan-Hispanic Congress in Madrid. This is a renewed manifestation of a long effort by Spain to serve as a loving mother country, culturally and otherwise, to the Latin-American states. This Hispanism is not highly dangerous, but it shows the need of alertness against totalitarian influences with supposedly Catholic sympathies.

Against the favorable information that Mexico will probably renew diplomatic relations with Britain within a month stands the apparent stagnation of the negotiations with the United States concerning oil expropriation. Mexico offers a token payment of $9,000,000 with later settlement of balances to be negotiated, which the oil companies reject in view of their original claim for $450,000,000. This difference in evaluation delays hope of the global settlement of difficulties which had been hoped for.

President Ávila Camacho pleased Ecuador and the liberty-loving peoples by his utterance before Congress that "Mexico will not recognize conquests by force in any part of the world." This declaration was recently matched by that of the president of Cuba that his country was openly committed to the foreign policy of the United States and considered itself an ally of England and Russia. The Cuban inhospitality to Arnulfo Arias, deposed Panaman president, indicates that the recent shift of power may escape the charge that it was a United States machination.

The labor situation in Latin America is marked by rivalries of mutually hostile groups. Lombardo Toledano's Confederation of Laborers of Latin America is meeting competition from a revived Pan-American Federation of Labor once sponsored by Samuel Gompers. Within Mexico itself the Confederación de Trabajadores Mexicanos is in conflict with the Confederación Revolucionaria de Obreros Mexicanos. Thus labor in Latin America continues to live in much the same dream world as it does in the United States; the short vision of labor leaders who hope to gain new advantages for labor while the form of society upon which labor subsists is menaced is one of the ominous signs of modern decay, which is augmented in its seriousness by often uncompromising attitudes of employer groups.

In brief, the situation in Latin America is highly fluid with opposition of political groups. While some of these confusions are purely national, many are concerned with world conditions. In Uruguay, in Chile, in Panama, Cuba, and Mexico, there are indications that the official and the popular support is on the freer and saner side of the conflict. In the Argentine, Colombia, and Peru there are grave dangers; in huge Brazil the pro-Nazis are for the present quiet; there is a general disturbance of the labor world. The vast economic stresses in Latin America have nowhere obtained adequate easing. But with the popular attitude almost everywhere anti-Nazi, the short-range perspective is as favorable as the expectation of ultimate Nazi defeat permits. In the longer perspective, with and after our own victory over the common enemy, the prospect is distinctly favorable for a Pan-Americanism allied to and coöperative with the trend of civilization, and of the world organization which is imperative.

If the status of America is truly associated with that of Europe, it will help to organize thought if we look for a moment at the trends visible in our old home. Germany, once possessing two hundred thousand square miles and eighty millions of people, since 1939 controls three hundred million people on an area seven times larger. Some twenty nations have lost entity. More civilians have died since 1939 in Europe than in 1914–1918. Millions of children have no parents, millions of families have no homes. The next steps of conquest run: Russia, North Africa, Great Britain, the United States, and, to the east, China and Japan.

The general countenance of Europe shows lines of suffering from hunger and deprivation and debasement, gifts of the Nazi domination which have brought revolts in Norway, Holland, France, the Balkan states, and elsewhere. Retributive executions of suspects and hostages by thousands in half a dozen countries prove that ruthlessness, coupled with griping fear, dwells in the hearts of the conquerors, who have snatched away food, clothing, and even bedding from their disarmed victims as a necessary preliminary to the establishment and operation of the benefits of the "New Order." Whether or not the continental revolts can be articulated with a new British western offensive is a matter of popular and parliamentary debate, not yet of action. Probably no great offensive in the west can come before spring. Hovering in the background is the fear of epidemics, such as the influenza which numbered its victims by millions in 1918. Famine, terror, and pestilence are visitors probably to be received during the coming winter in all Europe. They may not confine their incidence to the Old World.

Turning to particular nations once great, free, and independent, but now in low estate: there is pitiful France, France of the great republic and the wide-sweeping empire, the empire stripped of value in the hands of opposing factions, and the republic cleft in twain, half slave and half under the iron heel, each part awaiting a day of deliverance from its own Old Men of the Sea, a day believed in by every decent French heart, wherever the dispersal and however tenuous the hope. There is Italy, like a grounded airplane, minus the struts of its once flighty navigator. There are once-proud imperial Spain and Portugal, hanging in trembling fear to the toppling brink of the abyss which borders great Germany's geopolitical world island, endured by Hitler as Europe's last bridgehead to a world not yet his. There are the Scandinavian states, only one of them still retaining nominal sovereignty, and the others, with Holland and Belgium, under the bombs of the RAF, awaiting a day when a reconquest launched from Britain will see them again restored to entity by clanking columns of rescuing tanks and shaded by swarms of liberating planes. There are the Balkan states and Turkey, in varying stages of revolt, resistance, and reluctant obedience, with no heritage but fear and apprehension from either side.

And what of Russia? The decision to attack Russia on June twenty-second has been partially admitted as a mistake by Hitler, in that he did not realize the amount of preparation which had been made by Stalin; on the liberal side there was too little appreciation for the now demonstrated capacity of the Russian army to prolong resistance by a mobile defense in depth. Russia has held together not for six weeks, but fourteen. Such tenacious resistance, it was thought, would compel immobilization of gigantic German forces on the eastern front, and make possible some definitive action by the British on the west. But Russian demands that Britain strike are being met with irresolution and delay. Very possibly the organization of a grand movement to invade the Continent is beyond available British shipping; undoubtedly Dunkirk and Crete have taught ample if not overmuch caution. Possibly a blow is under organization in the southeast as an alternative.

Certainly the conquests made within the Russian frontier by the Germans have created a possibility of reorganization of the Ukraine and its resources so as to create new German strength to counteract recuperation of power by Great Britain on the Atlantic. Deprivation of ocean imports will be offset when the new territory comes into renewed production after its devastation. If internal supply can be developed, the struggle at sea cannot yield the destructive might over Germany which the blockade intended to accomplish. Even so, the withdrawal of the Moscow government to Sverdlovsk, where the iron and coal resources of the Ural-Kuznets regions may still be available, may make it impossible for the Germans to so stabilize their victories as to make them able to organize the resources acquired. The Russians might keep on fighting indefinitely if British and American help as promised should become sufficiently available. If German announcements of success are true enough to constitute threats of what they may accomplish within a few weeks, the opportunity given to England to create a western diversion will have been lost, and the time will be prolonged during which the American continent and the people of the United States must suffer dislocation of life before the final defeat of Germany is accomplished.

There must have been, too, some guaranties given by Russia regarding further world revolution and cessation of Bolshevik propaganda in America and the British Empire. Even a promise of no separate peace would be grounded on the kind of help Russia may get. The reëstablishment of peace on a secure basis in eastern Europe cannot be left to Hitler and Stalin in the·end. It is a world problem which may call for our own assumption at a later day of joint responsibility there. Isolationist orators could lash themselves into a fury at the prospect. Yet, if Russia can retain political entity and sovereignty under the principles of democracy declared in her

Constitution of 1936, she may be able to coöperate with the Americas, the British Empire, and with China to control the middle eastern strip of Europe which has been the bone of contention between Russia and Germany. This would be preliminary and preparatory to some organization of the world which will have to consider all regional issues as only parts of the whole. In such a settlement the United States must be vitally interested. But she cannot expect adequate representation in councils seeking working solutions of world problems unless she shares with all the struggling powers, including Russia and Germany, the responsibility for bringing the peace to pass.

Finally, the European picture is rounded out by Great Britain and the component British Empire. After enduring horrible punishment with superhuman courage, the British are quivering with the decision whether to offer a serious counterblow on the European continent. Are there ships and supplies enough, support from the Americas in sufficient stream and quantity, and assurance enough of continental coöperation by conquered peoples to warrant an attempt at establishment of a western front? Apparently not even the British who clamor for action can answer. Possibly, with Russia continuing resistance, large-size undertakings at various points on the periphery of German tenure, if rapid and decisive, might disconcert the Germans sufficiently to weaken the campaigns in the east to the point of exhaustion. To do this, British action would have to be quicker than seems at the moment possible, and it is not certain which side would be most assisted by winter, hunger, and pestilence. Diversions by Japan in the

Orient or the Pacific, or sudden shifts of governments in Latin America are elements of both the short and the long hazard; in all these the United States is vitally concerned. No moment of relaxation of will, planning, and execution can come to the British or to any of the liberty-loving peoples of the Americas until the yet unstopped Germans and their divided and bedeviled Oriental allies are defeated and bent to the determination of the peace- and liberty-loving world "to live quietly."

Space lacks here for more than passing allusion to some of the Oriental phases of the gigantean complex of world issues. It will suffice to say that Japan, after four years of inconclusive campaigns, finds herself not an entirely free agent of her destiny. She may choose to give up in China, or lose. Potent, like Germany, to destroy, she cannot escape her geographical insularity. Standing as she does, like Great Britain, on the periphery of the great world island or triple continent of the geopoliticians, her fate is bound up with the political and economic development and organization of that huge geographical entity as an underling of Germany if Germany wins. But, unlike England, Japan has no ally in the Western Hemisphere; on the contrary, her alert rival, the United States, is at long last denying her the *matériel de guerre* which she relies upon, although furnishing it at capacity limits to Japan's present enemies, Russia and Britain. And whether Germany wins, or Russia, Japan will have to use more adroit diplomacy, or more successful military and naval effort, to avoid satrapy under Germany or absorption by China. On this side of the world, when the Orient begins to migrate, as once did the Occident, the empty spaces of Latin America may prove so alluring that our western neighbors will find need of closer union to restrict the movement and preserve their peoples from too rapid conglomeration of stocks and disruption of societies. Except for her cohesive fanaticism and her present war machine, Japan has over Latin America no assurance of superior economic or political integrity.

Now then, amid all these uncertainties which span the globe in space, and with roots into the past reaching indefinitely into the future, what of Pan-Americanism? Naturally, with democratic victory, it must be what the United States and her associated Latin-American powers make of it. The United States needs Latin America badly, both for culture and for commerce, but in neither need can her word be fiat nor her processes those of absorption. In the existing nicety of the balance in the world crisis the fate of the continental concept depends now as never before upon the resolution, the good sense, and the present success of the foreign policies of the United States. Far more disastrous than loss of Latin-American markets and imports would be the erection of half a dozen Italys or another France or Belgium at our doors, with puppet dictators mouthing Hitlerian threats, promises, and insults over our radios. Good Neighborhood would be relegated to a distant future, and though the falsities of totalitarian societies would fall of their own iniquities in the long run, it would be such a very long run.

What, then, must the United States do in the emergency? First of all, we must face reality. Whether or not we are at war or "short of war," we have a situation in which we must fight; probably we can make the war long or short as we will and act. And if we win, as win we must, we can by judgment and will make a worthy and enduring peace.

To such an end our immediate need is to come unanimously to the support of the President of the United States in all his policies, foreign and domestic, which give vitality to happy government of our own people and strength and support to our liberty-loving neighbor states in Latin America, and to our associates under aggression throughout the world. Declarations and messages won't stop enemy subs, tanks, or planes. Shooting them at sight is dissipation of effort and prolongation of struggle; whenever we are able to take the initiative, at that moment war on the subs should go all-out. Their nests along the coasts of Europe must be hunted out and destroyed; airplane factories must be put out of commission, tanks and their factories destroyed, armies disorganized and beaten. Wherever troops would be practically useful, they should be sent, at the dictate of war strategy, not of ignorance or sentiment. The will to world domination must be exorcised, and the will to unity under law and coöperation under organization must be implanted.

Our own faults are copied in Latin America and elsewhere too readily. They are like the weaknesses which led France over the abyss. Opposition in our country to world-wide liberation is worse than apathy; it is active defeatism. Our sons become weak-kneed in seeking to elude reality.

When a mother of courageous heart speaks for vigorous use of our man power and is met by the query, "But have you a son?" she is being assailed by defeatism. When the query becomes a campaign, it is disloyalty. The suitable answer is,

"Yes, and I want him to be strong enough to face the world as he finds it, and be counted on the right side whether he stands or falls." When I am told that Hitler doesn't want world power, but only seeks to beat the British, I ask, "Where are your eyes?" If gentlemen continuously assail and decry policies adopted and actions taken with the votes of majorities in Congress and approbation of the people, I fear that mental atrophy and political ambition have become two complicating diseases annulling reason. When a self-selected orator tells the world that he is busy thinking up ways whereby the President may be hated into a fourth term, I regard his first farewell address with composure and gratitude—that virtue expectant of continued benefits!

There is one more point on which the United States must set a better example for Latin America. Both Latins and North Americans are beset with labor difficulties arising from strikes, lockouts, and disagreements of many kinds. This is a disunion of society which runs close to the pattern followed in Germany, Italy, France. Labor confusion in defense inevitably slows down the production of matériel; in other fields, as well as in war industries, the cost of increased wages in successful strikes falls upon the public more severely than upon the investor, most severely upon the white-collar class. For the present moment the peril comes in lack of preparaiton for a probable war; in the proximate future it comes with inflation.

When I think of our country in its present apathy and its coming plight, I remember the words of Nathan Hale: "My only regret is that I have but one life to give for my country." Or the taunt of Patrick Henry: "Is life so dear, or peace so sweet, that they must be purchased at the price of chains and slavery? I know not what others may think, but as for me, give me liberty or give me death." He was talking about a family quarrel, not about a struggle to save the lives of a score of nations. Now and again someone says for us: "I'd rather die on my feet than live on my knees." But aren't we living on our knees now? Think over your daily activities and your plans, listing those not modified by the war we call European, and then reflect on the fifty-three billions we are spending on it without having struck a blow in our own name anywhere! Where does peace end and war begin? How near does the moment draw when our leader will be forced to say to us: "I have tried to save you this, but now all I can promise you is 'blood, and sweat, and tears' "?

www.ingramcontent.com/pod-product-compliance
Lightning Source LLC
Chambersburg PA
CBHW052011270326
41929CB00015B/2878